# Born to SHOP

## ITALY

**Fourth Edition**

Bantam Books of Related Interest
Ask your bookseller for the books you have
  missed.

# Born to SHOP

## ITALY

### Fourth Edition

▼

**SUZY GERSHMAN**
and
**JUDITH THOMAS**

Introduction by
**ATHOS PRATESI**

**BANTAM BOOKS**

NEW YORK • TORONTO • LONDON
SYDNEY • AUCKLAND

## TO OUR CHILDREN

Although every effort was made to ensure the accuracy of prices appearing in this book, it should be kept in mind that with inflation and a fluctuating rate of exchange, prices will vary. The prices in this book were calculated at the exchange rate of 1,200 *lire* = $1 U.S.

BORN TO SHOP: ITALY

*A Bantam Book / April 1986*
*Bantam Second Edition / April 1987*
*Bantam Third Edition / February 1989*
*Bantam Fourth Edition / March 1991*

*Produced by Ink Projects*
*Design by Lynne Arany*
*Maps by David Lindroth, Inc.*
*Cover art by Dave Calver*

ISBN 0-553-35251-2

*Published simultaneously in the United States and Canada*

Bantam Books are published by Bantam Books, a division of Bantam Doubleday Dell Publishing Group, Inc. Its trademark, consisting of the words "Bantam Books" and the portrayal of a rooster, is Registered in U.S. Patent and Trademark Office and in other countries. Marca Registrada. Bantam Books, 666 Fifth Avenue, New York, New York 10103.

PRINTED IN THE UNITED STATES OF AMERICA

FG     0 9 8 7 6 5 4 3 2 1

# The BORN TO SHOP Team:

reported by:
Suzy Gershman
Logan Bentley
original reporters of first edition:
Suszette Gallant
Suzy Kalter Gershman
Carolyn Schneider
Judith Thomas
editor: Jill Parsons
executive editor: Toni Burbank
assistant to executive editor: Linda Gross

## Acknowledgments

Well, we've done it again. And we did it just for you. But we couldn't do it at all, without some help from our friends:

Hugs, kisses, and lots of thanks to Logan Bentley, our on-the-spot, right-there-in-Italy, *Born to Shop* reporter, who keeps us in the know. Her daughter Barbara Lessona also helped out.

Thanks to everyone at CIGA who helped out in a million ways with advice and train reservations. Special thanks to Enza Cirrincione and Carla Gaita in New York, and to all the concierges around CIGA's Italy who whispered their best secrets in our ears.

And, as always, thanks to our family and to the gang at Bantam who make it all possible.

# CONTENTS

# Preface

This new edition of *Born to Shop: Italy* has some changes in it that we'd better tell you about right up front. We've always loved the country look, adored Ralph Lauren, Colefax & Fowler, and Pierre Deux and disdained modern furniture for any reason beyond academics. But to our surprise we found that on this trip we flipped for Italian design and postmodernist chic. So get ready, folks; we've added a section on Italian design in Milan that we think will get you as hooked as we are.

We also confess that as we visit and shop in Italy, we are appalled by the high prices and the touristy crowds. We love Florence—but oh boy, in season is it a mess! So we've come to rely on Milan more and more for our shopping pleasures. This is the design capital of Italy; this is where business people do business— so there are fewer tourists. This is where prices are probably best, although we admit, prices all over Italy are high.

With Logan Bentley's help we've stayed on top of what's new and we've updated this entire book. But as you read, you'll find that we are concentrating more and more on Milan because Milan offers so much more for shoppers. Year after year as we return to Milan we become more and more convinced that Milan is the best "serious shopping" city in Italy. Note we didn't say best city in Italy—we love all of the cities for their ideas, inspirations, and charms, and we think it's impossible for any one to be the best. Milan is just the county seat of design.

As with all our books, certain rules apply:

▼ No store can purchase a listing in this book or in any book we write.

▼ Most of the stores we visit do not know we have visited them as reporters; it's all done incognito.

▼ All opinions expressed in these pages are strictly ours; we count on our reporters, but we still check out everything they say. If we give an opinion, it is ours, and ours alone. And we are very opinionated.

▼ As the series grows, we have begun to cut back on some of the more obvious listings (like all those Benettons) in order to give you more special, more *Italian* listings. We have Benetton in this book, but we don't give you every single store address.

▼ The books are not meant to be encyclopedias of the area; we just want to point you to what we consider to be the best stores and the best neighborhoods, and tell you how to get the best buys.

▼ This book is being revised constantly, but if you catch a change before we do, please write to us: *Born to Shop,* Bantam Books, 666 Fifth Avenue, 25th floor, New York, NY 10103.

# Introduction

To me, Mrs. Gershman and Mrs. Thomas have an impossible job. There are so many beautiful things for sale, how can you pick which ones go in the book and which ones don't go? Italy is such a breathtaking country, how can you limit a book to just four cities when you could write books on each of these cities and then more books on the countryside in between them?

A very hard job.

But they have done it very well. I asked them if they wanted the name of the store that made the best chocolate in the world; the best salami. "No," they told me. Did they want the name of the cobbler that made the most incredible slippers, lined with mink? "No," they told me. The best yachtmaker? "No." What they wanted was for me to invite their readers into my factory, to my little seconds shop.

They said they knew exactly what their readers wanted and that salamis and bedroom slippers were very nice, but their readers wanted big-name bargains. They want to buy the sheets they can buy in Beverly Hills and New York in Rome and Florence, and they want to know how much they are saving. Then they want to come to the seconds shop to rummage through the damages to see if there is anything else they must have.

I said I had to think about it. After all, I have a very good international business. What would happen if I gave away all this information? The more I thought about it, the more I started to laugh. People know that Pratesi means quality. It is human nature to try to get a bargain. Those who shop in Europe have always done so first for fun and then to save money. They will never substitute damaged merchandise for the real thing, because they respect quality too much. So, in the end, I realized that the factory outlet shop is there to sell what is there. Because the money made in the seconds shop helps the factory workers, the sales can only help. So I said, "OK." It is OK to help the factory workers; OK to let *Born to Shop* readers know we have some seconds, since they already know everything in our retail stores is perfection . . . Pratesi style.

We've had some changes in our store addresses in the last two years, and you'll be pleased to see that this new edition will help you find your way to our beautiful wares. We are always happy to offer wonderful Italian shopping to you, whether at a Pratesi store or at our factory.

So I welcome you to Italy, my country; to Florence/Pistoia and Milan, the cities I live in; to wonderful shopping from the best designers in the world; and to all the beautiful choices you have in every city. *Comè bella!*

Athos Pratesi<br>
President, Pratesi

# 1 ▼ WELCOME TO ITALY

## Shopping in Italy

Streets filled with water . . . pearls made of glass. But who cares when you're shopping in Italy? In fact, if that's not charming, what is?

Sure, there are some problems with shopping in Italy, and we want to address them up front, like adults:

▼ It's hard to tell the imitation Louis Vuitton and Gucci from the real thing.

▼ It's hard to pass up another great pair of $50 shoes, even when you don't need any more shoes.

▼ It's awful when you find something on sale in Milan after you just bought it at full price in Venice.

▼ It's rough when you have to face city after city offering fabulous choices that would wipe out even the Aga Khan's clothing budget.

No doubt about it, shopping in Italy can be difficult.

But give us more.

We've found that some of the most difficult things about shopping in Italy are the choices involved. We are torn between our first love—clothes—and wanting to see all the new, hot interior and industrial design ideas. And it's torture to know when to buy what. Tourists who go to Italy usually plan on visiting several cities. This means less time in a city, and even more choices. But we're not complaining.

Every place you go in Italy, you'll find style.

The Italians' ability to set aside the traditional and adapt to the new is mind-boggling. The result is spectacular and stimulating: When you shop, you run head to toe with hills as old as the ages, peeling *palazzi* with tile roofs and handmade wrought-iron gates and window grilles, masterful antiques, and then whammo—smack in the middle of it all—tables perched precariously on bent triangles, clothes in hot colors created from warm fabrics, and a pride of craftsmanship in absolutely everything.

## Best Buys of Italy

L ately the *lira* has fluctuated between 1,100 and 1,200 to the U.S. dollar. Yes, lunch can easily cost $50, and hotel rooms can be steep—but there are many deals that make it all a lot easier to afford. The same with clothes and gift purchases.

The average price of goods in Italy, especially clothing, is outrageous. Italians have smaller wardrobes than Americans do. Italians like to have one new fashion item, of good quality and in this season's color. They will wear this one item to death and team it up with everything else in the closet, weeding out only last season's hot color (which they will sell at a resale shop). They do not mind paying top dollar for top goods, and will pay even more for American-made goods. Because Italians are willing to pay for Italian design, good quality, and high fashion, they don't even understand why Americans expect to find bargains.

So you really have to be sharp:

▾ Resale shops are popular in Milan. The best ones take items that are only one year old (no more), which means they are viable choices for Americans—since many American designs are one year behind Italian fashions.

▼ Discounters are popular everywhere. While brand-name goods are always welcome, many Italians wear the preppy English look (made in northern Italy) but are happy to find the same fashions made in the Orient and sold at discount in Italy. An Italian's idea of a great discount shop may be one that just sells plain old V-neck sweaters.

▼ Private business in the home is a growing trend from Rome to Milan. Because prices are high, and there is some pressure to have a few hot items for each season's collections, middle-class women are meeting in friends' homes to buy wholesale. Unless you have friends in these cities, you're out of luck for this type of shopping.

▼ Fake Louis Vuitton has invaded Italy. There's not a woman who isn't carrying some kind of Vuitton bag—fake or real. Our favorite scene is the truck driver we saw get out of his truck, in his blue coveralls, and stand in the Customs line at the Italian-French border. On his left was his German shepherd dog; on his right— his Louis Vuitton briefcase. If you must have such a status item, the flea markets of Italy (and the street vendors) can make you happy for less than $50.

▼ Handbags, shoes, and leathergoods are still good buys in Italy. While prices might at first strike you as higher than at home, look carefully at quality. You'll pay more for a quality bag, but it will last for a very long time. Consider classic styles that you can enjoy for ten years (if they get scratched you can have them professionally redyed). But you needn't buy big-name to get a bargain. Quality should speak for itself.

▼ Pottery is a good buy in Italy, although you do need to worry about shipping. Buy from well-known resources if you plan to ship. Or buy one great piece you can carry on the plane.

▼ Costume jewelry is one of Florence's best buys. You'll find good costume jewelry all over Italy, and at very good prices. But when people ask us about buying gold in Florence, we just laugh. The days of the $6 earrings are gone, but you will find a lot of well-priced costume jewelry in stores, in markets, and even on the street. One of our best finds is an artisan from Bologna who spends his Sundays selling his one-of-a-kind pieces on the Ponte Vecchio.

▼ Scarves are good buys in Italy. The duty-free shops at the airports all sell scarves, although the selection can be spotty. But the fact is, these airports sell duty-free Hermès and Chanel scarves in the first place—these items are very hard to find outside of regular retail sources. While the duty-free savings is just 18%, that's good enough for us. If it's not good enough for you, compare with the scarves on airplanes or at street markets.

▼ Don't buy cosmetics, perfumes, regularly priced ready-to-wear, or Swatch watches in Italy—or any goods imported to Italy. Italians love British and American goods, but they pay very high prices for these things.

# The Moscow Rule of Shopping

The Moscow Rule of Shopping is one of our most basic shopping rules and has nothing to do with shopping in Moscow, so please pay attention. Now: The average shopper, in his pursuit of the ideal bargain, does not buy an item he wants when he first sees it, because he's not convinced that he won't find it elsewhere for less money. He wants to see everything available, then return for the purchase of choice. This is a rather normal thought process. However, if you live in the Soviet Union, for instance, you know that you must buy something the minute you see it, because if you hesitate it will be gone. Hence the title of our international law: the Moscow Rule of Shopping.

When you are on a trip, you probably will not have the time to compare prices and then return to a certain shop; you will never be able to backtrack cities, and even if you could, the item might be gone by the time you got back, anyway. What to do? The same thing they do in Moscow: Buy it when you see it, understanding that you may never see it again. But since you are not shopping in Moscow, and you may see it again, weigh these questions carefully before you go ahead:

1. Is this a touristy type of item that I am bound to find all over town?

2. Is this an item I can't live without, even if I am overpaying?

3. Is this a reputable shop, and can I trust what they tell me about the availability of such items?

4. Is the quality of this particular item so spectacular that it is unlikely it could be matched at this price?

If you have good reason to buy it when you see it, do so.

*Caveat:* The Moscow Rule of Shopping breaks down if you are an antiques or bric-a-brac shopper, since you never know if you can find another of an old or used item, if it will be in the same condition, or if the price will be higher or lower. It's very hard to price collectibles, so consider doing a lot of shopping for an item before you buy anything.

# City Planning

I f you are going to a variety of Italian cities, you probably are wondering which one offers the best price, the best selection, and the best value. There are no firm rules—the Moscow Rule of Shopping really applies—but we have a couple of other helpful (but loose) rules to guide you.

▼ *The City of Origin Axiom.* This is very simple: An item usually is cheapest in the city where it's made or where the firm's headquarters are. That's because the trucking and distribution costs are less. We may only be talking a matter of pennies, but we are betting on the best prices and the best selection in stores that are close to factories. Following this rule, Pratesi linens should be bought at the store in Florence, Fendi in Rome, and Krizia in Milan. For the most part, shopping in Rome is not as good as in other Italian cities.

▼ *The Milan Rule of Supply and Demand.* If we don't know the city of origin for an item, or want to be safe, we use the Milan Rule of Supply and Demand. Because Milan is the center of the fashion and furnishings business, it should have the best selection of big-name merchandise. It may be a few *lire* more expensive than in Venice, but the sales are immense, well-organized events, and you are dealing with retailers who are in the business of moving goods—they make better deals. Milan also is far more industrial than the other big cities. Its entire psychology is one of moving and selling goods and services. Venice and Florence are crammed with tourists, especially in summer months, and the shopkeepers are very aware of you as a tourist. We've never thought shopping in Rome was such a big deal, so we vote for Milan ... for selection and, especially, for sales.

▼ *The Better Market Theory.* If you like to buy imitations or are a market buff, the best buys are in the street markets. Florence has the best street market (San Lorenzo, see page 165). Nothing in any other city (except maybe San Remo on a Saturday) compares. You can do all your shopping in Italy in an hour in the San Lorenzo market, if you are not an Uptown Girl.

## Be Prepared

We thought we left homework behind the day we graduated. But the bargains go to the shopper who is ready to recognize them, and that means doing some homework:

▼ If you have favorite designers or targets of acquisition for your trip, shop the major department stores and U.S.-based boutiques (if in your city) for comparison prices. Don't assume you will get a bargain on an Italian purchase.

▼ If you do not live in a city that has a lot of European merchandise, do some shopping through *Vogue* and *Harper's Bazaar.* In the ads for the designer boutiques, you'll find phone numbers. Call and ask about prices and sales. Don't be afraid to explain that you are contemplating a shopping trip to Europe and are doing some comparison pricing.

▼ Read Italian magazines to get familiar with looks, shops, and lifestyles. While they cost a fortune, many libraries have these magazines. We go to a hair salon sometimes just to read the European magazines.

▼ There are no bargains on perfume or cosmetics in Italian stores. Buy these items at the duty-free at the airport when you leave, or in France, or at home.

▼ The best buys in Italy are on designer merchandise on sale that fits into your suitcase and into your U.S. Customs allowance.

▼ If you shopped in Italy in the dollar's glory days, you may be shocked at the current high price of merchandise. Everything is expensive, even cheap merchandise. Don't go expecting bargains without understanding where the bargains are. Know your stuff before you leave home. If on a tight budget, buy imitation Vuitton and call it a wrap.

▼ Be prepared to buy little but to soak up ideas galore. Carry a notebook; tear pages from magazines. Carry a tape measure if you are considering home designs.

# 2 ▾ DETAILS

## Watch Out!

I f you're looking for a deal that's just too good to be true, you may find one—and it will be a scam. For a scam to work, the victim must be naïve enough to allow it to work. When you are in a foreign country, when you're on vacation and wanting to believe in magic, when you cannot speak a language, you are vulnerable to scams. Most of them are small-time shopping scams, but they are annoying nonetheless, and expensive if you get taken.

Reputable shops (and hotels) usually are safe. But even in classy establishments, be careful when you talk to strangers. We've met some wonderful people in hotels and on airplanes around the world, but there is a rather well-known scam in which the con artist pretends to be just the kind of person you'd like to know and then whammo, takes you for a ride. Remember:

▼ Merchandise, especially name merchandise, selling at a price that is too good to be true is usually too fake to be true.

▼ If a person volunteers to go shopping with you, to steer you to some real "finds," to help you find some long-lost family members of yours, or whatever—don't trust him! There are more tourist scams of this nature in Italy than anyplace else except maybe Hong Kong. Be safe . . . not sorry.

▼ No matter how well-dressed the person is; no matter how friendly the person is; no matter how helpful and endearing—the answer still is "No." If such a person is following you or becomes a real nuisance, call the police, duck into a prestige hotel and ask the concierge for help, or walk right into the American embassy.

▼ Likewise, if a person volunteers to take your money and buy an item for you cheaper than you could get it because you are an Ugly American, forget it. If you want the concierge of a reputable hotel to handle some shopping for you and you know the hotel well enough to trust the concierge, by all means, do so. (Don't forget to tip for such a favor.) Otherwise you are taking a risk.

▼ Always check your purchases while they are being packed by the store, and when you return to your hotel, unwrap them to make sure you got what you thought you were getting. Mistakes occur, but occasionally someone will switch merchandise on you. Return to the shop the next day if an error has been made. Bring your sales slip. If you anticipate a language problem, have the concierge call the shop for you and explain the situation, then have him tell the shop when you will be in for the proper merchandise.

▼ Don't forget the old newspaper scam. A poor person (or two or three) spots you with an attractive shopping bag. He is reading or holding a newspaper as he passes you on a crowded street—or worse, on a bridge. The newspaper passes over your shopping bag while the thief's hand goes into your bag for the goodies. The person reading the newspaper may or may not be the thief—this scam is worked by mothers with three or four children in tow. We've also heard it worked so that the person reading the newspaper passes you, grabs your glasses, and then runs off while several children pounce on you, take your shopping bags and handbag, and dash off while you are wondering what hit.

▼ Don't forget the old *metro* trick. You know the one, where some "boys" pick a fight among themselves between subway stops—your pocket is picked and they are out the door before you know what has happened.

▼ Don't forget the old *Mamma Mia!* scam. You are involved in a transaction being conducted in Italian, which you barely speak. If you question the mathematics, the vendor rolls his eyes, waves his arms, and screams at you. You feel like an idiot and leave, not wanting to cause a scene. You have just been cheated out of $50 in correct change. Congratulations.

## Booking Italy

We have specific information on hotels in each city section, but we also have a general announcement: Most travel agents can sell you an Italian Hotel Pass. This is for any type of hotel (even the ultra-deluxe CIGA chain). The price of the card varies with the class of hotel you pick and the number of nights you buy, but the per-night rate is considerably less than if you booked that very same hotel on a regular basis. Call Maiellano Tours (800-223-1616 or 212-687-7725) for an Italian Hotel Pass if your regular travel agent can't get you one.

## Getting There

Several airlines fly to various Italian cities, and it is not at all hard to get to Italy from the United States. But if you are coming from another European country, we suggest a few tricks. Use the train by combining your passes. A complete Eurailpass may be too much for you, especially if you are just visiting two countries (say, France and Italy). If you use a French Rail Pass and an Italian Rail Pass, you can get from Paris to Rome without more cost than that of the two passes. This is the least expensive way to get to Italy. If you take a sleeper, you will pay an extra fee for the wagon-lit (this varies by destination but is about $50–$60). If you go with a couchette, with five other people in the car with you, the price drops to about $15 . . . one-way.

# Getting Around

We have been using Italian trains for years and swear by them. We can't imagine driving around Italy when you can take a train to the big cities and then get a car for only a day to explore the countryside. While train fares from city to city (especially in second class, which is how we travel), are not expensive, we recommend that if you plan to travel extensively around Italy, your best buy is an Italian Rail Pass, which can be bought in the United States (Italian State Railways, 666 Fifth Avenue, New York, NY 10103). This pass costs a flat price for a certain number of days and is good for unlimited mileage and all trains, including the faster ICC (intercity) trains and the *rapido*. We are so sick of being asked for *supplementi* (additional payments beyond the cost of the ticket) each time we buy a new ticket to get on a train that we find the one-price comprehensive pass to be a godsend.

If you want to drive, use an American-based car rental plan, which will be half the price of Italian fees at the same agencies. Fly-drive packages offer the best prices.

# Finding an Address

A ddresses all over Italy can be confusing. Some follow the European tradition—a building has a single number, and all stores share that number. Many addresses are written with the abbreviation *ang,* which stands for "angle" and means "at the corner of." An address with an angle often has no number, only two street names.

Also, there are several hidden messages in the color of the numerals on the buildings in Italy. Each city has a color for house numbers; in Florence the numbers on buildings come in black or red—red is for retail establishments, black is for residences.

# Shopping Hours

T he shopping hours in Italy are similar to those in all European cities: Shops open at 9 or 9:30 A.M., and they close at 1 P.M. for lunch. They reopen at 3 or 3:30 P.M. and stay open until 7:30 P.M. Some stores will close on Saturday at 1 P.M. Stores open on Saturday afternoon are closed in the summer. In most cities some stores stay open at lunchtime —places like Upim and Standa.

Keep track of local holidays and religious holidays (when you check into a hotel, always ask the concierge immediately if there are any holidays approaching and how they will affect the banks and stores!), since shops will close tight then. Different cities celebrate religious holidays with differing amounts of piety. Shops that are closed in Rome may be open in Milan.

(December 8 is a big holiday in some towns, a medium holiday in others.) August 15 is a big religious holiday, and all stores are closed.

August is also the official beginning of the summer vacation season. Most shops in Milan, and many in Rome, too, close between August 1 and September 1. Shockingly, some stores close for a longer time. Our beloved Il Salvagente, a discounter in Milan, closes for six weeks in the summer (July 15 to August 30).

## Hotel Shopping Deals

Some hotels in Europe now offer special shopping discounts to their guests. Inter• Continental hotels have a special program for VIP guests. CIGA hotels have a program for all their guests; it's called the CIGA Shopping Card and is good for shopping in the four major Italian cities—Milan, Venice, Florence, and Rome.

▼ If the reception desk does not automatically give you a shopping card and explain it to you, ask for one. All registered, paying guests at a CIGA hotel qualify for this courtesy.

▼ You will get a black cardboard credit card that is called the CIGA Shopping Card; you sign it, just like any other credit card. Sometimes the concierge signs it or writes his initials, so shopkeepers know it's genuine. It has an expiration date on it, and each card is numbered and stamped.

▼ With the credit card you'll get an accordion-style folded brochure that lists about a hundred stores in the four major cities and that states whether you will get a discount or a gift (omàggio) with purchase. The usual discount is

10%, but if you use a credit card you will get only 5%.

# Italian Duty-frees

We have had a love-hate relationship with duty-free stores in airports for years. We love to visit them. We get to the airport early, just so we can wander through them. But we hate to buy anything, for fear that we are not getting it at the lowest possible price. We have researched this over many trips and many years, and have discovered that the only way to score in a duty-free is to know your airports and your merchandise.

So we are thrilled to tell you that the duty-free stores in Rome (Leonardo da Vinci) and Milan (Malpensa), which are owned by the same company, are winners. Not everything in them is a bargain—those Pringle sweaters are outrageously expensive. In fact, imported items probably should be ignored by Americans. And if you order your perfume from Catherine, the duty-free in Paris, you may do better on some perfume prices. But if you want it in your hand immediately, buy scarves, candy, booze, and Italian designer items at the duty-free stores.

The Rome airport has one of the best duty-free setups in the world: There are several shops that sell a variety of merchandise, from sporting goods to high fashion to the more traditional liquor, cigarettes, candies, and toiletries. We found about an 18% discount on Trussardi, on Enrico Coveri, and on Ferragamo shoes, and while we might not be so bold as to tell you to save all your shopping for the airport, we do suggest these airports for last-minute gifts.

Not every shop in an airport selling area is a

duty-free (or, more accurately, tax-free; you still must pay duty on what you buy in a "duty-free"). Not every shop offers a bargain. Many of these stores are outrageously expensive; some just charge the going rate. Remember the candy bar story: we priced the exact same candy bar at the Milan train station (3,000 *lire*), at the duty-free in Milan (1,400 *lire*), and in the airport shop next door to the duty-free in the Milan airport (2,200 *lire*). Unfortunately, designer goods aren't usually kept in stock like candy bars; but you get the idea.

Some tips:

▼ Liquor prices are good in Italy's duty-frees.

▼ Candy prices are also good in Italy's duty-frees, but the selection of Italian brands is spotty, and you may actually do better at an American discounter.

▼ Foodstuffs make nice gifts, and the duty-frees have a lot of them, from Harry's spices and sauces (called Arrigio in Italian, but from the same famous Harry as in Harry's Bar) to dried mushrooms and noodles, which are allowed into the United States. Prices are moderate on these items, and since you can't get them anywhere else, they become especially attractive.

▼ Scarves are discounted, including Chanel and Hermès, which are hard to find at discount prices anywhere in the world (18% discount).

▼ Ties are cheaper in the United States—try Dollar Bill's, 99 East 42nd Street, New York, New York, for Italian designer ties under $15. They are $25–$40 in the Italian duty-free stores.

▼ Don't forget that whatever you buy at the duty-free must be declared when you return to the United States. Unless you eat it on the plane.

▼ And never forget that duty-free shopping no longer ends when you leave the airport duty-free. All airlines now have duty-free shopping on the plane. The price list should be inside the in-flight magazine. *Buon viàggio.*

## Finding Fakes

T he more famous the name brand, the bigger the problems with counterfeiters. In the various markets we visit we see a lot of merchandise that seems to have "real" canvas but "fake" bindings. Look at stitching and metal fixings on leathergoods from Gucci, Vuitton, or Fendi to tell if they are real. Also check the quality of the stamping on the canvas and the way the logo letters are formed.

In the less glamorous area, watch for imitation Kodak camera film. You'll see the familiar Kodak box and logo, only to discover on careful examination that you have bought a cheap rip-off labeled Kolak—but the *l* and the *d* look quite similar.

## Italian Perfumes

W hile the French have the reputation, not only for their perfumes, but for their duty-frees—which sell fragrance at fabulous discounts to Americans— you might want to be the first on your block at home to try some of the Italian designer fragrances. You won't get a great break on prices; you might not find the very obscure ones in the duty-free stores at the airport. However, you may find something no one else has, if you just keep on spritzing. Try: *Teatro Alla Scala*

by Krizia, *Echo* by Mario Valentino, *Roma* by
Laura Biagiotti, *Il Profumo* by Nazareno
Gabrielli, *Diego Dalla Palma, Via Condotti* by
Lancetti, *Polidori Donna,* or *Curiel.*

## In the Bag

S hopping bags are freely given at boutiques
and department stores when you make a
purchase. Not so in grocery stores. Either
bring your own with you or expect to pay
about 50¢ per plastic sack. The large can of
olive oil that you came to buy comes with a
handle, so you might not even need a bag.

## Bar None

T his is not strictly a shopping secret, but
each person we tell this to is so shocked
that we figure we ought to pass it on to
you. If your shopping becomes too much
for you and you think you'd like to wander
into a bar for a coffee or a snack, please note
that all bars in Italy have two systems: Either
you order at the bar and stand and drink at
the bar, or you order at a table and you eat
seated at the table. To eat at a table will cost
just about double the price of a meal at the
bar. It is rude and unacceptable to order at
the bar, pay at the bar, and then wander to a
chair and sit down!

# Department Stores

There are two types of department stores in Italy, and stores of each type have branches in most major cities. The big stores loosely based on the English system of department stores are La Rinascente and Coin. They are traditional department stores. Then there're Standa and Upim—both are postwar variations on the traditional department store and are more like discount stores in the United States—not unlike K mart.

We sound so blasé about all this because the Italians themselves just don't like department stores. Italian women of style, fashion, and money want service and quality. They want small specialty stores where they are known, and where they get personal attention. Italians don't like self-service, they don't trust department stores, and they want personal contact.

If you understand this, the department stores can be put into perspective. They aren't bad. They just aren't great. There's no such thing as a Macy's or a Bloomingdale's. There's not even a Galeries Lafayette. La Rinascente is as good as it gets. And there's nothing wrong with La Rinascente—its private-label merchandise is excellent.

Standa and Upim also are good choices if you like inexpensive merchandise, or if you have kids and need underwear, socks, a quick bathing suit, or some emergency clothes. Get inexpensive panty hose at either resource. But women who shop only top-of-the-line stores will not like these resources.

# To Market, to Market

O ne of the difficulties of shopping in Italy is deciding which markets to visit and which to pass up. Unlike most other countries, whose cities usually have one or two good markets, Italy is crawling with good markets. There are actually dozens of them, and it's impossible to get to them all unless you spend a month doing little else.
Remember:

▼ Dress simply; the richer you look, the higher the price. If you wear an engagement ring, or have one of those wedding bands that spells out RICH AMERICAN in *pavé* diamonds, leave it in the hotel safe.

▼ Check with your hotel concierge about the neighborhood where the market is located. It may not be considered safe to go there alone, or after dark. Beware Rome.

▼ Have a lot of change with you. It's difficult to bargain and then offer a large bill and ask for change. As a bargaining point, be able to say you have only so much cash on hand.

▼ You do not need to speak any specific language to make a good deal. Bargaining is an international language of emotion, hand signs, facial expressions, etc. If you feel like you are being taken, walk away.

▼ Branded merchandise sold on the street may be hot or counterfeit.

▼ Go early if you expect the best selection. Go late if you want to make the best deals, pricewise.

▼ Never trust anyone (except a qualified shipping agent) to mail anything for you.

In Florence and Rome, most market areas are so famous that they have no specific street address. Usually it's enough to name the market to a cabbie; but ask your concierge if you need more in the way of directions. Usually buses service market areas.

# Shipping from Italy

S hipping anything from Italy begins before you get there. If you are smart, or serious, you will do some homework before you leave, and have your shipping arrangements partly made before you even arrive. You'll complete the transaction once you arrive in Italy, and then you'll have (you should excuse the expression) smooth sailin'.

Sure, you can be wild and crazy and walk into a store and buy a container's worth of furniture you hadn't planned on buying—but we don't think too many people do business that way. Instead, contact a shipper in your hometown, or in New York, and work together to make sure all your shipping days are pleasant ones. The shipper should be able to act as your agent—the buying game will be much less tense once you have someone to take care of you.

▼ When you arrive in town, plan to meet with your chosen shipping agent. Make the appointment from the United States, and meet with the agent as soon as possible so you can feel confident and on top of things.

▼ Explain to your agent the kinds of things you are planning to buy and the approximate number of pieces. Tell him if it's valuable antiques, merely used furniture, original Michelangelo canvases, or what. Discuss a cost estimate and make sure you have a complete understanding of how the system works and how much you are paying per cubic meter (about $200 is the right price, by the way). Ask about groupage in a container or whether you should have your own container.

▼ If you can't fill a container, ask how long you will have to wait for space in a container. This could be a long wait.

▼ Discuss the connections to be made from New York to your hometown. Ask if the package is indeed shipped through New York, or through another port city, which may be closer to you. New York gets more packages; this routing probably will save you time. The proper shipper should be able to arrange direct shipping.

▼ Find out if you need a customhouse broker to meet your goods and clear them, or if the shipping agent does this. Is this part of the shipping cost, or is there an additional fee?

# U.S. Customs and Duties

To make your reentry into the United States as smooth as possible, follow these tips:

▼ Know the rules and stick to them!
▼ Don't try to smuggle anything.
▼ Be polite and cooperative (up until the point when they ask you to strip, anyway . . .).

Remember:

▼ You are currently allowed to bring in $400 worth of merchandise per person duty-free. Before you leave the United States, verify this amount with one of the U.S. Customs offices. Each member of the family is entitled to the deduction; this includes infants.

▼ You pay a flat 10% duty on the next $1,000 worth of merchandise. This is extremely simple and is worth doing. We're talking about the very small sum of $100 to make life easy—and crime-free.

▼ Duties thereafter are based on the type of product. They vary tremendously per item, so think about each purchase and ask storekeepers about U.S. duties. They will know, especially in specialty stores. Note that the duty on leathergoods is only 8%.

▼ The head of the family can make a joint declaration for all family members. The "head of the family" need not be male. Whoever is the head of the family, however, should take the responsibility for answering any questions the Customs officers may ask. Answer questions honestly, firmly, and politely. Have receipts ready, and make sure they match the information on the landing card. Don't be forced into a story that won't wash under questioning. If you tell a little lie, you'll be labeled as a fibber and they'll tear your luggage apart.

▼ You count into your $400 per person everything you obtain while abroad—this includes toothpaste (if you bring the unfinished tube back with you), items bought in duty-free shops, gifts for others, the items that other people asked you to bring home for them, and—get this—even alterations.

▼ Have the Customs registration slips for things you already own in your wallet or easily available. If you wear a Cartier watch, you should be able to produce the registration slip. If you cannot prove that you took a foreign-made item out of the country with you, you may be forced to pay duty on it!

▼ The unsolicited gifts you mailed from abroad do not count in the $400-per-person rate. If the value of the gift is more than $50, you pay duty when the package comes into the country. Remember, it's only one unsolicited gift per person.

▼ Do not attempt to bring in any illegal food items—dairy products, meats, fruits, or vegetables (coffee is OK). Generally speaking, if it's alive, it's *verboten*. We don't need to tell you it's tacky to bring in drugs and narcotics.

▼ Antiques must be at least 100 years old to be duty-free. Provenance papers will help (so will permission actually to export the antiquity, since it could be an item of national cultural significance). Any bona fide work of art is duty-free whether it was painted fifty years ago or just yesterday; the artist need not be famous.

▼ Thinking of "running" one of those new Italian handbags? Forget it. New handbags shout to Customs officers. They can spot you coming. Honest.

# 3 ▾ MONEY MATTERS

## Paying Up

**W**hether you use cash, traveler's check, or credit card, you probably are paying for your purchase in a currency different from American dollars.

For the most part, we recommend using a credit card—especially in fancy stores. Plastic is the safest to use, provides you with a record of your purchases (for U.S. Customs as well as for your books), and makes returns a lot easier. Credit-card companies, because they often are associated with banks, may give the best exchange rates. The price you pay as posted in dollars is translated on the day your credit slip clears the credit-card company (or bank) office, not on the day of your purchase.

The bad news about credit cards is that you can overspend easily, and you may come home to a stack of bills. If currency is fluctuating wildly and the dollar happens to fall, you also end up paying more for your purchases than you planned. The day you walk into Valentino and blow your wad on a suit, you walk out thinking you have paid $600. Three days later the paperwork is done on your charge slip, and if the dollar has fallen you may end up paying $650.

On the other hand, the one extra benefit of a credit card is that often you get delayed billing, so you may have a month or two to raise some petty cash.

Another advantage to using credit cards is your purchase may be protected. The American Express Card offers Purchase Protection. This plan, automatic with every card, assures you of extra insurance coverage for the first ninety days from the purchase date if the item you bought (with your card) is lost, stolen, or accidentally damaged. Remember to save all receipts. You must prove the purchase date and the fact that you used your American Express Card, although you can always call Amex for your "record of charge." American Express also offers Buyer's Assurance. This plan extends the warranty of any purchase up to one extra year.

All credit-card companies have similar programs; check with each one individually to find out the rules before you go. Some companies ask you to sign up for the program; some plans are only for customers with "gold" cards. Call the main number for your bankcard and ask.

Traveler's checks are a must—for safety's sake. Shop around a bit, compare the various companies that issue checks, and make sure your checks are insured against theft or loss. While we like and use American Express traveler's checks, they are not the only safe game in town. BankAmerica provides traveler's checks in various currencies, and for $5 more gives you an insurance package that is wonderful. Thomas Cook provides traveler's checks free and in foreign currencies. American Express can provide traveler's checks in *lire*, but you most definitely will pay for this privilege. This is a big plus when changing checks at hotels or shops, because you will have a guaranteed rate of exchange. However, you must buy the checks through a bank, Deak-Perera, or another currency broker, who may not give you the same rate of exchange as the American Express office abroad.

## Cash and Carry

I f you must carry cash with you, use a money belt or some safety device. We use Sport Sac zipper bags, which are large enough to hold passport, traveler's checks, and cash.

We won't tell you where we secure them, but our valuables are not in our handbags, which can be rather easily stolen, or around our waists, since this can be uncomfortable. We've heard of extra-large brassieres, under-the-arm contraptions, and all sorts of more personal and private inventions. You're on your own here—but do remember to take care.

# Currency Exchange

A s we've already mentioned, currency exchange rates vary tremendously. The rate announced in the paper is the official bank exchange rate and does not apply to tourists. Even by trading your money at a bank you will not get the same rate.

▼ You will usually get a better rate of exchange for a traveler's check than for cash, because there is less paperwork involved for banks, hotels, etc. However, CIGA hotels give a better rate for cash.

▼ The rate of exchange you get is usually not negotiable at a given establishment. Hotels do not give a more favorable exchange rate to regular patrons, etc.

▼ Do not expect a bank to give you any better rate than your hotel, although they may. We've generally found the best rate of exchange at the American Express office. Usually they give as close to the bank rate as is humanly possible. Most banks charge a commission to change money, so hotels may be competitive . . . and easier.

▼ If you want to change money back into dollars when you leave a country, remember that you will pay a higher rate for them. You are now "buying" dollars rather than "selling" them. Therefore, never change more money than you think you will need, unless you stockpile for another trip. At the airport in Rome, you must have the original receipts in order to get dollars for *lire*.

▼ Keep track of what you pay for your currency. If you are going to several countries, or must make several money-changing trips to the cashier, write down the sums. When you get home and wonder what you did with all the money you used to have, it'll be easier to trace your cash. When you are budgeting, adjust to the rate you paid for the money, not to the rate you read in the newspaper. Do not be embarrassed if you are confused by rates and various denominations. Learn as much as you can, and ask for help. Take time to count your change and understand what has been placed in your hand. The people you are dealing with already know you are an American, so just take it slowly. Use a calculator to avoid being cheated.

▼ Memorize comparative rates for quick price reactions. Know the conversion rate for $50 and $100 so within an instant you can make a judgment. If you're still interested in an item, slow down and figure out the true and accurate price.

▼ If it's all mind-boggling, use our easy method. Figure the dollar at 10 rather than 12 and get an instant fix on prices. Lunch for 39,000 *lire* costs slightly less than $39, etc.

## Cash Machines

Cash machines are taking over the world and are extremely popular in Europe, just as they are in the United States. There's just one catch: The machine in Italy probably will not take your card.

American Express has its own little machines, which will take your cards if you are registered for this service and have your own special number. This service will probably spread so that in future years you can get money anywhere you go abroad, but don't count on it now. MasterCard and Visa cards now work at some machines.

## Personal Checks

It's unlikely that your hotel will take your personal check, unless they know you very, very, very well and you are (a) famous, or (b) rich, rich, rich, or (c) both. Be prepared to cry, whine, or go to extraordinary lengths to get your hotel to provide this service. But carry your checkbook anyway, because all sorts of other places will take your old-fashioned American check (couture houses, for example).

The best bets are mom-and-pop stores where the owners are anxious to have funds in a U.S. bank account; since the amount of money they can take out of Italy is limited, they never deposit the money in Italy.

You will also most likely want to write a check to U.S. Customs to welcome yourself home. We always do.

Never travel without your checkbook!

## Send Money

You can have money sent to you from home, a process that usually takes about two days. Money can be wired through Western Union (someone brings them the cash or a certified check, and Western

Union does the rest—this may take up to a week) or through an international money order, which is cleared by telex through the bank where you cash it. Money can be wired from bank to bank, but this is a simple process only with major big-city banks that have European branches or sister banks. Banks usually charge a nice fat fee for doing you this favor. If you have a letter of credit, however, and a corresponding bank that is expecting you, you will have little difficulty getting your hands on some extra green . . . or pink or blue or orange.

In an emergency, the American consulate may lend you money. You must repay this money. (There's no such thing as a free lunch.)

# Export Tax

Italy really does have an export tax credit, and you really can get it. If you've shopped in Italy before, we know you've just fallen into a faint. But quick, the smelling salts: The system has been revised recently and is working better now.

OK: Some countries have a system for crediting taxes back to shoppers who buy goods and take them out of the country. In France they call it *détaxe*; in England it's VAT—value-added tax. In Italy it merely is called the export tax; it has no other name we've ever heard. The amount of the tax credit varies in each country. It also may vary by category of merchandise; thus in France furniture gets an 18% *détaxe* credit, while perfume gets a 33% credit. England offers a flat rate, as does Italy. The Italian tax is 18%. After 1992 it is expected that a flat VAT refund will be offered. However, it's not clear exactly when after 1992 it will happen.

Until recently it was virtually impossible to get the export tax credit out of Italy. While the law was on the books, you were hard pressed to find a store that would give you the papers, let alone the deduction. But things have been changing and there is now some hope, especially with big-name stores. The minimum expenditure to qualify is currently 525,000 *lire*.

The export-tax system in Italy is by no means as sophisticated as those in France or England, but it does work. First things first:

1. When you see that you are about to make a purchase of over $500, make certain the store will give you the discount. Some stores will tell you that the $500 must be spent on one single item. A few stores will go by the total.

2. You must insist that two pressings be made of your credit card in order for you to get the credit on your personal piece of plastic. Many stores do not understand this process, and in the long run you will lose the battle. Expect a fee of $15 to be debited on your account if you use the credit-card method.

3. When you are at the airport, but before you check your luggage, go see the Customs officer. If you can't find him or her, you have thirty days to get the papers stamped by U.S. Customs and returned to Italy.

4. Mail the papers from the airport. We've done this only from Milan, but there is a post office attached to Malpensa (Milan International Airport). Usually there is a post office in any international airport. Pray that the Italian mail is working.

5. Your credit comes either as a credit-card credit (if you're lucky) or as a personal check in *lire*. Good luck.

# 4▼ ITALIAN DESIGN

## Italian Style

Few other societies have such a strongly linked architectural, furnishings, interior design, and fashion structure—one that stands on its own internationally. The very complication of who does what (Gianfranco Ferré once was an architect; most teapot designers are architects) leads to the glory that is Rome and Milan and Florence and Venice.

Italian style is very firmly either traditional or trendy—we call that look New Italian—but either choice seems to combine all elements of the lifestyle.

*Classical.* The classical look in Italian style, particularly in home furnishings, always has been sparse, because the size of the rooms in your basic Italian villa is so large. Ceilings are high, salons are big, and no one could possibly turn them into something cozy like an English cottage. The cluttered look the Brits love would never work, and even the semicluttered look that works in old French homes does not quite make it in Italy. The classical Italian *palazzo* is decorated in an eclectic manner with old furnishings, many of which have been handed down through the generations, but with a minimalist effect, which best shows off the actual architecture of the house. The look never has been lots of little picture frames on several end tables, nor are the antiques of one particular time period.

*New Italian.* Born after World War II, with the rebuilding of Italy, New Italian style began in the factories of Milan and then spread throughout Italy and the world. In home furnishings, the look came to be defined by the use of new materials and the acceptance of creativity and a kind of inventiveness—there was appreciation for the talents of a person who could add a new twist to an idea as old as the chair. In fashion, the same inventiveness was combined with construction, technology, and clear, clean color—even if the color was black, beige, or gray. The line became the look, and the rest became a matter of construction.

# Ready-to-Wear

Few new Italian designers are based in Rome anymore. Instead they flock to Milan. Many Italian ready-to-wear lines are created by French designers; many ready-to-wear lines are added to leathergoods companies that have made good—Ferragamo, Gucci, Fendi, etc. Some Italian designers have practically become French couturiers, since they only show in Paris.

Most of the big, recognizable names of Italian fashion—from Missoni to Benetton—are ready-to-wear names, with offices, showrooms, mills, and retail outlets most densely placed in northern Italy in one of the mill towns that populate the hills stretching between Turin and Venice, which include the Milan metropolitan area. Just as New York attracts those who want to be the leaders of the American fashion industry, so Milan houses designers from all over Italy who want to break into sew business.

Although there are stores everywhere, fashion and designer headquarters are in Milan, and that is where the fashion shows are held twice a year, just prior to the French *Prêt à Porter*—in late March (or April) and October. Buyers and designers of ready-to-wear from all over the world come to Milan not just to see these shows but also to walk the streets and pick up on the street fashions, the new ideas, the undiscovered talent. They also may buy items at random in boutiques, modify them through their own suppliers, and turn a small trend into a big trend. Buyers with a good eye and a sixth sense for a trend can judge which items can be brought through to become mass merchandise and which items will die on the street.

# Italian Designers

**GIORGIO ARMANI:** Gray-haired, blue-eyed Giorgio Armani is a fixture in the American fashion alphabet because of his strong position in international design. He has been called one of the top five designers in the world. Armani got his start designing menswear with the Nino Cerruti line. (He had been a menswear buyer for the department store La Rinascente.) He went off on his own with a partner (1974), then branched into women's wear, where he is credited with bringing a feminine version of the menswear look to women. His look always has been unstructured, soft, easy to wear.

He lives in a *palazzo* in Milan and designs Armani (black label), Armani GFT (white label), Mani, and Emporio. Currently there are numerous Emporio Armani stores all over the world. There are men's, women's, and children's lines as well as several fragrances and international licenses. The flagship Armani boutique is in Milan.

**BENETTON:** Benetton can only be described as a phenomenon. Based in Treviso, an industrial city near Venice (no canals, no gondoliers), the Benetton enterprise—which is family-run—churns out some two thousand designs a year. All those zillions of shops you see all over the world are owned either individually or in blocks by franchise holders. Their buyers buy directly and therefore choose their own selection, so the merchandise in each Benetton you visit is a different mix, and sale times and prices may vary. Prices are suggested, and few stores vary from these suggested prices. Benetton does what is called vat dyeing: As the warehouses run low on a color, or stores order a certain hot color, graygoods are dyed to fit the need. The children's line is called 012; other Benetton-owned lines are Sisley and Tomato. All lines are in the moderate price range.

**GIULIANA BENETTON:** Yep. She's from the famous sweater Benetton family, although that's not her in the ads you'll see in Italian fashion magazines. Who cares what she looks like in person, because her shoes are not only dynamite, they're also moderately priced. At last, something unique in Italy that you can afford. Look for the shoes at any Divarese shoe store in Italy.

**LAURA BIAGIOTTI:** Showing couture and ready-to-wear, Biagiotti is best known for her cashmere knits. In her cut-and-sew work, Biagiotti has been known to show a sense of humor. Many of her styles are loose and full—they make stunning maternity dresses and are nice on women with imperfect figures (as if any of us has an imperfect figure!). Her cashmeres are expensive, but sought-after.

**BYBLOS:** We're not sure if this design line should be classified as Italian or English—and we know many women who think it's French! The designers Keith Varty and Alan Cleaver are English, but the goods are made in Italy. Byblos is sold in specialty shops—the kind that usually sell Complice and Genny as well—and is a competitive ready-to-wear line. Byblos isn't as famous in America as it could be, mostly because the company has no splashy advertising campaign or freestanding stores. But Byblos crosses the line between traditional and trendy, sitting smack in the middle of the road for the person who wants to look safe but stunning.

**CALLAGHAN:** This is not an English or an Irish but a well-respected Italian line. Romeo Gigli has been a part of the company's success. Turn to Callaghan for well-made fashion with a flair. Prices are moderate for designer fare, but not inexpensive.

**ERREUNO:** Because of some confusion about this line in the past few years, we want to spell it all out for you. Erreuno SpA is a company that has its own line and its own retail stores. Up until recently the line was designed by Giorgio Armani, and was a way of getting the Armani look at a more affordable price.

**ETRO:** Gimmy Etro's family has been in the paisley business for centuries—with some of Italy's most famous mills, in the Lake Como area. The "new" Etro line is a line of "leather" goods made from vinyl, created in a traditional paisley pattern and trimmed in cognac leather. This wears like Vuitton, is considered quite chic, and is currently the rage of those who can afford it on several continents. Bergdorf Goodman carries the line in the United States. Also on sale in these stores are paisley linens and shawls—everything is deluxe beyond words and makes you feel like you're the kind of person who travels only on the Orient Express.

**GIANFRANCO FERRÉ:** Ferré is a former architect, and his work is identifiable by its construction and architectural lines. In addition to his ready-to-wear and various licensees, he also has a couture line. The store in Milan, which is the flagship, is gorgeous and of course very architectural. We think these are divine clothes, but more for the tall woman (the tall, rich woman) and not for the same customer who likes puffed sleeves and floral prints. If you are interested in construction, just look at one of those wool jackets. Ferré designs couture for Christian Dior, but continues with his Italian ready-to-wear.

**FENDI:** Fendi is a sisterhood of five women who run various aspects of the family business, which includes leathergoods, ready-to-wear, and furs. The furs—which are designed by Karl Lagerfeld—are fun and crazy. (Often you can get a Fendi fur on sale at Filene's Basement.) The series of shops in Rome is fabulous fun and worth seeing; the other Italian cities have nice shops that are small and usually teeming with tourists. You can buy something in a Fendi shop for as little as $25. Don't be shy about looking.

**GENNY:** Genny isn't a designer's name; it's run by a woman (Donatella Girombelli) who hires various designers to create for this line and several others that she owns. Almost every big-name Italian designer has at one time or other designed for this line, which is sold through its own chain of boutiques or through department stores. Prices are high.

**ROMEO GIGLI:** This young master of cut and drape designs his soft, romantic collections with dramatic flair. Only a few pieces of his adventurous line are totally unwearable. Stores are beginning to pop up internationally as he moves quickly toward fame and fortune. Could he possibly be aiming for French couture?

**KRIZIA:** No, Krizia isn't the designer's name—it's the name of a character from Plato. The designer behind it all is Mariuccia Mandelli, who has several licensees and creates many Krizia lines, including the Poi line, which is a little more affordable than the regular line. Highly imaginative and with a good sense of humor, Mandelli still manages to produce drop-dead elegant clothes that rich women wear. Almost all of the boutiques all over Italy look similar, with gray interiors with textured concrete and high-tech touches. The Milan store is the flagship. Mandelli's sister owns the Rome shop; the Venice shop is larger than the one in Rome and has a better selection. Remember, the Krizia Moods line is not sold in Europe.

**MISSONI:** A family venture, the Missoni firm is famous for its use of knits and colors. While the husband-and-wife team (now joined by their children) continue to do what they've always done best, they have become tied in with architect/designer Saporitti, who has designed many of their boutiques, including the one in New York and the one in Milan. The Milan shop is worth seeing as a piece of architecture and an incredible example of New Italian style. Prices of Missoni are high. We must announce, however, that only the Milan store (the main store) has sales at which merchandise is marked down 50% to 75%. These sales are at the end of the season and are worth the price of a plane ticket in terms of savings.

**MOSCHINO:** If you have a good sense of humor and believe that fashion should be fun, you'll love the work of bad boy Franco Moschino, who is what the French call a *créateur*—he does not do couture, but his ready-to-wear is so inventive it always makes waves. What Moschino does best is lampoon current fashion trends; his favorite target in recent years has been Chanel. Moschino now has his own shops, but is also sold in all the specialty stores that carry designer merchandise. Prices are moderate to high; the really wild stuff frequently goes on sale. You'll be amazed to know that Moschino is such a voice in Italian fashion that Coin department stores sell imitations of Moschino's imitations!

**OLIVER:** The big news around Italy (and around the world, for that matter) is the handful of Oliver stores that have sprung up—see them in Rome and Milan as well as in Hong Kong and Singapore. Oliver is the name of Valentino's pet bulldog, and the line is Valentino's interpretation of sporty and casual—a great look for those who can afford such stuff.

**LUCIANO SOPRANI:** Although you think you've never heard of Soprani, you're wrong. One of Italy's most famous designers—even before the Milan group got its name—Soprani has been the silent force behind many of the most famous Italian ready-to-wear lines. You've seen (and probably bought) his designs for Gucci ready-to-wear and for Basile. His men's clothes currently are sold at the ultratrendy Kashiyama.

**VALENTINO:** The famous designer Valentino, most known for his work in beige, is legally named Valentino Garavani. In some countries (e.g., Japan), licensed goods are registered in his legal name. These are not necessarily the man's own designs. If you want true Valentino merchandise, you buy it in Italy through either Valentino couture, ready-to-wear, or a shop that sells the ready-to-wear made by GFT (which says GFT in tiny letters on the label). These lines include Studio V, Miss V, and Night. Some Valentino shops sell GFT merchandise; others do not. There is little Valentino Garavani merchandise legally sold in Italy. Most cities have Valentino Uomo (menswear) boutiques.

**EL VAQUERO:** The El Vaquero look is the Italian version of the cowboy look in shoes, boots, and handbags. There are now some two dozen stores all over the world selling this pedigree version of the Marlboro man (or woman). The look is distinctive; once you know it, you can spot the designs ten meters away. Look for tooled leathers, insets of lace, multiskin ornaments, tassels, fringes, beads, medallions, and nailheads. The average pair of El Vaquero shoes will have a pastiche of five different elements all woven smoothly together into a piece of art. The look is very popular in Beverly Hills and Miami, as well as in Saint-Tropez—if that helps give you a fix. Sizes seem to run slightly small.

**GIANNI VERSACE:** Years ago, when the Milan group was just rising in the world of fashion, we were certain that Gianni Versace would lead the pack. We were wrong. Versace has totally sidestepped the pack. He does a look that no one else can do—it makes his clothes distinctive and amusing at the same time. One of the most inventive designers in fashion, Versace does a men's and women's line that is best characterized by its ability to be different—from the combination of fabrics and prints to the cut of the clothes themselves. Versace is shape and flair and humor. In most Italian cities, the men's and women's stores are separate boutiques.

## The French-Italian Designer Crossover

No, it's not your latest Robert Ludlum thriller. But the French-Italian designer crossover is a wonderful process to watch and profit from. Because Italy and France are so close, it's easy for designers to scuttle back and forth. Mariuccia Mandelli—the Krizia genius—tells stories of her early days when she got a little extra help from an old friend named Karl Lagerfeld, who flew in from Paris, worked all night with her, then flew back to Paris for the next day's work there.

Besides the crossover designing, there is crossover manufacturing as well. These lines, when bought in Italy, are high fashion at lower prices.

It's just been a pretty well-kept secret—most of the *haute* French (and also some Italian) designers create additional ready-to-wear lines that do not bear their names. Those sneaky devils! Everyone knows that Karl Lagerfeld designs the Fendi furs and was responsible for the double F design in the Fendi canvas. But who knows that Frenchman Thierry Mugler does an Italian line, fittingly named Allure? The Girbauds have a special line made in Italy and also produce a lot of their other goods here; Luciano Soprani has a cheapie line called Motivo.

## Boutique Lines

**B**ig-name designers have boutique lines that may not have their names on them. For instance, Mani, a boutique line by Giorgio Armani; or GFF, by Gianfranco Ferré, who often uses his initials or the name Oaks on his licensed lines. Ferré also does Studio 000.1. The Titolo line comes from Basile.

## Italian Specialties

**A**lthough pasta and cheap Westerns are Italian specialties, the ready-to-wear specialties are more regional. The industrialized northern part of Italy is most famous for its wools and its leathergoods. Not only are the wools famous, but almost all the fabrics are famous—especially the silks of the Lake Como region. Designers from all over the world come to Italian mills—or come to trade fairs to meet industrialists who represent the mills—to do business and buy sophisticated Italian yardgoods. Entire villages are known for their fabrics, or their yarns; others are known for their knits.

English-style fashions are another Italian specialty. You may be surprised by the preppy sweaters and styles. Most are very expensive.

Shoes are a good buy, as are the handbags, belts, and other small leathergoods Italy is famous for. Again, many internationally famous designers come into the factories and workrooms and create their lines, and then ship them home. We don't need to tell you that it's not unusual for a handbag made in Italy to have "Made in France" stamped inside it in gold letters.

Italian-made leathergoods—based on both the quality of the leather and the quality of the workmanship—are considered among the finest in the world. While less expensive leathergoods have found a place in the international market (especially in the United States), no other country can touch the quality of Italian-crafted items. As a result, the leathergoods market recently has specialized itself into the higher-end market. Currently about 200 companies export leathergoods into the United States—famous names such as Bruno Magli, Salvatore Ferragamo, and Fratelli Rossetti, and unfamous names who nonetheless compete with a high-quality item at a lower price. Many of these makers own their own shops. Bruno Magli has just opened up in California; Beltrami moved into Manhattan three years ago. Naturally, when you shop these stores in Italy, you can hope to save money.

You can also buy from the guys we call the no-namers—those makers and retailers who have no international reputation and whom we have never heard of. They aren't in *Vogue*, and they don't show in Rome. They just make a great pair of $50 shoes. And after all, isn't that what you came to Italy for?

# Italian Interior and Home Furnishing Design Qualities

**D**espite the encroachment of the French designers on what was solidly Italian turf, design mavens insist that there are certain elements that immediately shout "Italy!" and epitomize Italian style:

▼ industrial artwork;

▼ products that reflect a knowledge of design in other cultures;

▼ craftworks, one-of-a-kind types of design and detailing;

▼ unusual color and material combinations;

▼ experimentation with form;

▼ an ability to combine a traditional idea with something new; and

▼ architectural roots.

# Italian Home Design Today

The current trends in Italian home design began when France put the make on the international home furnishings market and came to the fore with a new group of hot designers who suddenly began winning contests and international job bids and making news with their ideas and creative persistence. Italian designers were amused and stunned— and also angry that after so many years as undisputed heads of creative design, now, rather suddenly, New French style and New Italian style should look so similar.

Italian designers are inspired by the classic looks of the 1920s, 1950s, and 1960s. The French are doing the exact same thing. Although the Memphis look got a lot of press, it was more popular as an export novelty than as a local design phenomenon. Now the entire Memphis look is considered passé by many rival firms who are concentrating on classics and basics rather than on gimmicks or gewgaws; Milano Nostalgic is hot now.

*One warning:* We have heard of Americans who love the Italian home furnishing looks and who have gone to the showrooms with designer credentials and big bucks to spend and ship, only to discover that some of the showrooms are feeling so confident of their talents that they are charging exorbitantly high prices. American distributors of the very same goods are charging less money for the same items in the United States, and the furniture is already landed—you don't have to worry about shipping. If you plan to shop for home furnishings, know your U.S. prices—wholesale and retail—and which local or New York discount stores carry this furniture. There are a few discount sources in Manhattan that often have New Italian–style looks that may warrant a trip to New York.

## Postwar Style

After World War II, Italy found itself in an intriguing architectural dilemma. Few buildings were still standing. Furthermore, there wasn't a lot of money with which to rebuild the country. Inexpensive, portable, modern furnishings and fixtures were called for. Due to lack of space, those people lucky enough to have homes were not necessarily lucky enough to have offices; the in-home office was born, and the crossover furnishings market, in which office furniture looked great in the home, and vice versa, was invented.

Because of the need to make all this stuff as quickly and inexpensively as possible, and because there wasn't enough money to build a lot of big buildings, two really interesting things happened:

▼ Architects began to design furnishings and accessories—since there wasn't too much work doing buildings.

▼ Italian designers (read architects) pioneered the use of plastics and then other inexpensive and newly developed postwar novelties, such as foam rubber.

By the early 1950s, Italy pulled away from the postwar international rationale of cheap furniture for the masses (which was also being produced in every other country) and began to specialize in a more exclusive kind of design, with more highly crafted detail and combining several materials—some cheap, some expensive—that was aimed directly at the high-fashion, high-style, high-priced market. No one has looked back since.

## Plastics, Benjamin

**P**lastics were the first materials that made Italian furnishings different, and they continue to be used in innovative ways. The Italians made plastic socially acceptable. In 1969, Massimo Vignelli designed a set of dinnerware for Alan Heller (Hellerware) that introduced two incredible new concepts to the American market: chic plastic for the dinner table, and stacking dinnerware. Both would revolutionize the tabletop market.

Of course, the first plastics were developed in the 1950s—the big industrial companies (e.g., Pirelli) had been working on the notion since before the war, and some of the new design firms, such as Kartell and Artemide, decided to specialize in the form. The plastics boom began with laminates that covered tables and cabinets, and then moved into molded objects as the technology evolved. With the wide acceptance of plastic as part of the new fashion, other new forms were developed to enhance the look or to reside with it in a state of grace—highly polished chrome became hot, especially in the world of industrial design (chrome coffee machines, etc.), leather-wrapped furniture evolved into its own look, antistructural design had a fling (the beanbag chair), and sculptured foam grew popular. High tech was born in the ashes of the war, but no one knew it yet.

# Crafts Revival

The glory years of New Italian furniture were from 1958 to 1962. By the late 1960s, various cultural movements changed furnishings fashion; by the early 1970s, the oil crisis affected the use of plastics, laminates, and poly-ersatz fabrications. By 1973 Italian design leaped into a crafts revival. Workmanship, detailing, individual styling, and privately commissioned pieces were the mode of the day. Architects and designers took to designing one incredibly imaginative piece that would be exhibited but possibly never put into mass production. Architects actually became artisans.

The English Arts and Crafts movement, Art Nouveau, the Glasgow School, and other craft movements of the 1920s had been gobbled up and forgotten in Italy after the war in the effort to go modern and cut off all links to the past. Yet as Italy eased away from the success of its modern period, designers found beauty and style in facets of the forgotten Arts and Crafts movement. This was coupled with an international fling at individualism and a greater recognition of the need to get back to basics, to appreciate fine materials and nature. While some of this philosophy still exists today, it was more important as the groundwork that led to the transition from modern Italian design to avant-garde design.

# Avant-Garde Italy

The emergence of high-tech, highly crafted individual pieces and pop art furniture in the early 1970s created the right breeding ground for the avant-garde movement begun with Studio Alchimia and carried on by Memphis. In 1980, Studio Alchimia achieved international notoriety with its furniture created from industrial materials in bizarre shops and handpainted with wild and sometimes punk-looking patterns. (The punk movement, which had begun as a frightening aspect of street fashion in London in the early 1970s, became more and more mainstream through the intervention of fashion and industrial designers who modified the look and brought a certain aspect of New Wave style into acceptability.) In 1981, Memphis (a design group of several famous designers from various countries, not just Italy) took gallery space in Milan and introduced their version of the look, which injected a sense of humor and presented furniture that was outrageous for the sake of being outrageous but still amusing, and still socially acceptable because it continued to function as furniture (even if it didn't look like furniture).

The reaction in Italy, amazingly enough, was mild, or minor. Few were truly amused or impressed. It was the international press that latched on to the two design firms, especially Memphis, and created the well-publicized sensation. Although the original Memphis pieces were merely prototypes, and although new pieces from the studio continued to be priced at astronomical sums that put them out of bounds for most people, the look was so well publicized that it affected designers all over the world and soon was copied and adapted to fit modern, mid-1980s lifestyles.

# The Creators

I f you are looking for the big names of Italian industrial and tabletop design, you will find their work either in the big showrooms or in the stores and showrooms operated by the large firms that have underwritten their designs. The names of the designers themselves are sometimes less well known than those of the distributors or big firms who gave them the push. Also remember that although the design comes from Italy, it may not have been designed by an Italian. Nonetheless, as you look in galleries, showrooms, and store windows, watch for some of these names:

▼ Knoll International, one of the most famous design distributors, pioneered the use of clean Italian design in both the office and the home. Very often, famous international designers will design a collection for Knoll.

▼ Rosenthal China (made in Germany) has many of its products designed by Italians. Mario Bellini is one of the more famous (he has been designing for Rosenthal for years), and his works are prominently featured in all Italian cities in stores that carry Rosenthal.

▼ Superstar architect/designers include Gae Aulenti, Gio Ponti, Carlo de Carli, Franco Albini, Pierro Pinto, Jonathan de Pas, Donato D'Urbino and Paolo Lomazzi, Joe Columbo, Marco Zanuso, Gastone Rinaldi, Carlo Santi, and Ettore Sottsass.

# 5 ▼ MILAN (MILANO)

## Welcome to Milan

Milan doesn't have the charm of Florence, or even the charm of Turin, but it is the city to visit if you are looking for Italian style, Italian inspiration, and new-fashioned fashions.

To tell the truth, we suffer from a love-hate relationship with Milan. As a city, we find it lacking in charm. As a shopper's delight, we find it Mecca. The more we visit, the more we begin to consider Milan the capital of Italy.

Milan does grow on you. While the city is far too industrial to ever be cute, it has a certain European flair that isn't charm but is nonetheless very real. When you're prowling the streets of Milan on a shopping spree you get an instant fix of fashion merely by looking in the windows. When you learn how to ride the tram you get a feeling of elation at having conquered a very special foreign city—your kind of town, after all. There's no doubt that Milan has become a major fashion center, a major convention center. It's no secret that international garmentos are turning up to find the goods they will tote to Hong Kong to have made into inexpensive copies. The Milanese streetcar may not be named Desire, but the designer goods are.

## Booking Milan/1

If you're serious about Milan, you might want to hightail it over to the Galleria, across the street from the Duomo, where there is a large Rizzoli bookstore with books in many languages, including English. Revisions can be sporadic, check the copyright before you buy. In English, there's *A Key to Milan*, published by Arcadia. This is a color-coded book with complete sections on all aspects of life in Milan, and it does include some shopping advice. Also look at *A Survival Guide to Milan* by Jill Stainforth, which is written more for those who will be living in Milan.

The books cost about $20 each but are very different from each other. If you're a regular to Milan, spring for both if you can.

## Booking Milan/2

We rate hotels in Milan as inexpensive (under $100); moderate ($100–$150); and expensive (over $150). Most offer a continental breakfast with the price of the room.

**CIGA 3:** CIGA, the famous hotel chain, has many hotels in Milan, but we call the three that are grouped together at Piazza della Repubblica the CIGA 3. They are the Principe di Savoia, the Duca di Milano, and the Palace. All three are fabulous hotels with equal locale; we rank them only in terms of status. If you are a movie star, a big-name designer, or royalty, you stay at the Principe. If you are a businessman, you stay at the Duca. If you are a gourmand, a celebrity not wanting to be mobbed, or a businesswoman, you stay at the Palace. The rooms in all three hotels are identically decorated—we know because we've stayed in all three. In each you get the usual elegance of a CIGA hotel and a good location down the street from the train station, you are within walking distance of the main shopping district, and you get a CIGA shopping card, which is good for discounts in many Milan stores. For reservations from the United States call (800) 221-2340. Expensive.

**HOTEL PALACE**, Piazza della Repubblica 20 (Telephone: 6336)

**DUCA DI MILANO**, Piazza della Repubblica 13 (Telephone: 6284)

**PRINCIPE DI SAVOIA**, Piazza della Repubblica 17 (Telephone: 6230)

▼

**JOLLY PRESIDENT:** This is a businessman's hotel, and a great find because it's modern and deluxe and yet its location at Largo Augusto is next door to Via Durini, with all its designer shops, and one block from the Duomo, which can be seen from your window. A wonderful location for shoppers. There is another Jolly, which we happen to like a lot, called the Jolly Touring, which mostly caters to groups. It's not as fancy as the President, but it has a great location between Piazza della Repubblica and the shopping district. Jolly hotels are much more like staying in a foreign hotel than CIGA, and may be difficult for some. Expensive.

**JOLLY PRESIDENT**, Largo Augusto 10 (Telephone: 7746)

**JOLLY TOURING**, Via Tarchetti 2 (Telephone: 6335)

▼

**HOTEL MANIN:** If you want a little hotel that has a small lobby and a great location, think about Hotel Manin, which is across the street from the park (Giardini Pubblici) and right at the edge of the prime shopping district. In fact, it's next door to the Jolly Touring. Decorated in the 1950s Italian style, this hotel is a favorite of buyers and fashion journalists who come for the collections. Moderate.

**HOTEL MANIN,** Via Manin 7 (Telephone: 6596511)

# Getting Around

G etting around town on public transportation is not hard if you can stand the traffic in peak hours. The *metro* system does not get you everywhere you want to go, but the tram and bus system is very good. You must buy tram or bus tickets at a tobacco stand (marked with a *T* sign out front) before you get on the vehicle. Enter from the rear, and place your ticket in the little box machine to get it stamped. Keep it; you can use it again within seventy-five minutes. *Metro* tickets can be bought in the station; there are change machines, since you will need coins to operate the ticket-making machines.

Milan's *metropolitana* is supposed to have three lines, but one line seems to be stuck in the middle. You'll notice the rubble when you emerge from the Centrale train station. It is a big topic of conversation in Milan as to when, or if, that line will be completed. There *are* two lines—a red line and a green line; tourists will find the red line most convenient, as it does go to some of the major shopping areas and also stops at the Duomo. Look for the giant red *M* that indicates a station. Many guidebooks have a *metro* map printed inside them, including the freebie brochure your hotel will give you called *A Guest in Milan.*

The tickets for the tram and the *metro* are good for a set time period (seventy-five minutes), within which you can come and go without buying more tickets.

You can take a train to nearby communities, such as Como or Bergamo, or even to Venice, for a day trip. There's a large commuter population that goes to Turin, mostly for business, but you can go to shop or to see the Shroud. If you want to get to out-of-the-way factory outlets, you'll have to rent a car or hire a car and driver. You might not save any money, but you'll have a great time.

# Snack and Shop Milan

**AL NAIF:** One of our favorite places for lunch, or dinner, in Milan is a little hole-in-the-wall restaurant on the edge of the main shopping district, next to the Giardini Pubblici and just down the street from most of the hotels in Milan. We continually return for the moderate prices, homey atmosphere, and country cooking at a fine location at the Piazza Cavour where Via Manzoni meets Via Senato, just one block from Via della Spiga. Reservations probably are not necessary, but, just in case, the telephone number is 792167.

**AL NAIF**, Via Senato 45

▼

**CAFFÈ MODA DURINI:** In the Moda Durini shopping center, right on Via Durini, you can drop by for strong coffee and little snack items. Not much in terms of a real lunch, but good for a pick-me-up and very convenient.

**CAFFÈ MODA DURINI**, Via Durini 4

**SAVINI:** One of many cafés inside the Galleria, this one is the "in" place to be seen. Eat or snack, while shopping or after the opera; look for celebs and smile. Verdi ate here; so did Hemingway. You're in good company, so don't slurp the pasta. Not cheap. Reservations: 8058343.

**SAVINI,** Galleria Vittorio Emanuele II

▼

**BICE:** Chic luncheon spot where the designers hang out, right in the heart of the shopping triangle. Reservations: 702572.

**BICE,** Via Borgospesso 12

# Neighborhoods

## The Golden Triangle

All of the big designers have their gorgeous and prestigious shops in this nice little area of town that you can cover in a day or two or an hour or two, depending on how much money or how much curiosity you have. This is the chic part of town, where traditional European design flourishes along with Euro-Japanese styles and wild, hot Italian New Wave looks. It includes a couple of little streets that veer off the Montenapoleone; some are closed to traffic to make strolling even more fun. This is where you find the Ferrés, the Fendis, and the Krizias of the world. There are also some very tony antiques shops here.

There are showrooms to the trade that are so fancy and so secluded that you would never know they are there, and there are plain old retail shops (such as our find for sporting goods, **BRIGATTI**) that service plain old people.

# Milan

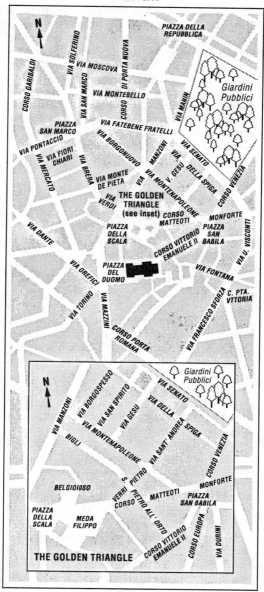

The outermost borders are Via Manzoni and Corso Venezia—these are big commercial drags. Use them mostly for finding your way; they are not top priority for shopping. Your real shopping streets will be Via della Spiga, Via Sant' Andrea, and Via Montenapoleone.

These three are the higher-rent streets of this promised land, but please don't miss the several other streets in the area. You will pass them anyway, so weave along Via Gesù, Via Borgospesso, and Via Manzoni (see "Antiques," page 94).

## Duomo

The Duomo is an incredibly detailed and gorgeous church. It is not a store. It is on a square—Piazza del Duomo—and is considered the city's main landmark. All directions and meeting places are arranged in relation to the location of the Duomo. But around the Duomo—aha, there you have it—is a leading shopping area. The Via Montenapoleone struts off Corso Vittorio Emanuele II. Two neighborhoods—Golden Triangle and Duomo—back up on each other, connect, and can easily be shopped together as one.

Jutting out of the back end of the Duomo is Corso Vittorio Emanuele II, which is filled with big stores, little stores, and about half a dozen galleries that house even more stores. The most maddening part about this area is that you can hardly find an address. No matter; just wander in and out and around from the Duomo to Piazza San Babila, which is only two or three blocks. At San Babila, turn left and you'll end up at Via Montenapoleone for entry into the Golden Triangle.

At the front end of the Duomo, off the *piazza*, is a shopping center, the Galleria. It has a vaulted ceiling and looks like a train station from another, grander, era. Inside there are restaurants and bistros where you can get a coffee and sit and watch the parade. Several big-time shops are here, including a **PRADA** (handbags, shoes, leathergoods), a **RIZZOLI** bookstore (books in English), and a tourist center. The Galleria is set at an angle. If you go out the back side, you will be at La Scala. Behind La Scala is the Brera area.

## Brera

Milan also has a lower-rent area—the part of town where the new guys can break into retailing and high style. We call it Brera, in honor of the main street with the same name. It's a good but not hard walk from the Duomo.

Via Brera is the tail end of Via Solferino. Solferino is the up-and-coming street of the district—it is about 50% developed and gains new shops every day. This is one of those streets that American department store buyers love to prowl because they can discover new talent.

The sneaky thing about Brera is that it really has two different personalities. The main stretch of Brera is rather commercial and even teenage— lots of jeans stores and stuff like that, as well as very obvious branches of the famous names: **LAURA ASHLEY, SOULEIADO, NAJ OLEARI**—but behind all this, there are the kind of back streets that are closed to vehicular traffic, that are narrow and bewitching, calling you to explore them and to press your nose to the glass of each shop. Many of the stores are the most expensive antiques dealers in the city; some of them are the ateliers of up-and-coming designers. Every now and then you just find a great, cheap shoe store. There are designer shops in here also: **Il BISONTE** is here, as well as **ANGELA CAPUTI**, both on the Via Madonnina (Caputi at No. 11; Il Bisonte at No. 10). Don't miss **ETRO** at Via Pontaccio 17, at the corner of Vicolo Fiori. Being in this part of Milan is like being in a different city. It's rich, it's elegant, it's secret, it's special, it's centuries old, and it's oh, so romantic. The best way to see it is during the Brera antiques street fair (third Saturday of each month; see page 98), when vendors have tables out in the narrow streets and a well-heeled crowd browses. But any day is a good day. Prices are better than in the Montenapoleone area, and the charm is greater. Don't miss Via Fiori Chiari and Via Fiori Oscuri and the entwining streets. The edge of the district is a wonderful street called Via Mercato—aptly named, because it has a fruit and vegetable market as well as several little greengrocer and *trattoria* places where you might want to get a snack.

On Via Solferino, stop in at **GALLERIA MICHEL LEO** (No. 35), a gallery-*cum*-antiques shop that specializes in 1950s tabletop; **CARTA-BALO** (No. 29), the best paper art of the most unusual sort; **GUARDA ROBA** (No. 9)—Teen angel, can you hear me? **URRAH** (No. 3), an Italo-Japanese-Americano sporty shop; **MICRO BRERA** (No. 23), gorgeous high-tech art glass; **CONTROBUFFET** (No. 14), the craziest store you'll ever see, very Milano and hip; and **ACCADEMIA** (No. 11), a men's store that is famous for being ahead of its time.

And on the Piazza San Marco, try **MIRABELLA** for linens, duvet covers, robes, and specialty Italian house and home goodies at reasonable prices.

## Buenos Aires

Corso Buenos Aires is a "real people" street, but it's fun. There are old department stores that are sort of decaying. But someone got wise to the area and brought in the new talent, so there are also hot new shops and places to discover. If you are a serious shopper, if you prefer to pay the best prices, if you can live without the luxury and the charm of the Golden Triangle, this is your kind of neighborhood.

Teens and their moms: First stop is Buenos Aires.

Corso Buenos Aires officially begins at the Oriental Gate, which once was the beginning of the commercial road for the Republic of Venice. Today the Corso is almost a mile long and features over 300 shops—it is one of the most concentrated shopping areas in Continental Europe. Many designers have other shops in this area—such as **GINORI** and **T&J VESTOR,** as well as **BENETTON**. There are tons of bars, cute restaurants, markets, and fabric shops. Avoid shopping on a Saturday if you can—it's mobbed. Remember, this is where the real people shop, so few people will speak English. The clientele is not always chic. You'll find at least three Benetton shops in various guises in the neighborhood; we prefer these to the fancy ones in the chic part of town. Remember that Sisley and Jeans West are both Benetton names, as is Tomato. Begin to stalk your bargains at the Porta Venezia and work to the Piazzale Loreto. Many of the shops have no numbers—often the number by a store represents the block rather than the store address, so many shops may be called "3"—but it's all easy once you're there. Just wander and enjoy; you can't miss the good stuff. Oh, yes, there's even a newly renovated **STANDA** and an **UPIM**.

You can get there easily by taking the No. 65 streetcar from the Centrale train station and getting off at Corso Buenos Aires (about three stops—everyone else will get off there, too). Or take the *metro* to Loreto and walk toward Venezia. Don't miss:

**DRUGSTORE:** This trendy little shop has rock music blaring and reminds us of San Francisco in the good old days when we were young enough to wear the clothes being sold at this shop. It's fun, it's kicky, it's well-stocked, and it's cheap.

DRUGSTORE, Corso Buenos Aires 28

**LULU:** Lulu is more inviting from the outside than Drugstore and is a fun, creative shop with lots of possibilities. It reminds us of an Italian version of Ann Taylor. Prices are less expensive than at Drugstore and lots less expensive than at Ann Taylor.

**LULU**, Corso Buenos Aires 3

▼

**MAMA NOEL:** Bright neon yellow and white diagonal stripes distinguish this young, hip, and stylish shop for mothers and babies. You name it and they've got it. This is a great place for that unique baby gift with the Italian high-fashion look.

**MAMA NOEL**, Corso Buenos Aires 23

▼

**BUENOS SPORT:** A great place to stock up on your Fila. We compare prices back and forth here with Kappa Sport, at No. 72.

**BUENOS SPORT**, Corso Buenos Aires 4

▼

**SOGARO:** This is one of the older, more traditional fabric shops, but it sells designer fabrics, towels, sheets, etc. Most everything is upstairs, but downstairs we once found Liberty of London at hefty discounts.

**SOGARO**, Corso Buenos Aires 17

## Navigli

South of the Porta Ticinese is the canal area of Milan. The canals have been built over, so don't spend too much time looking for a lot of water (wait for Venice), but the Navigli, as they are called, are fast becoming their own little neighborhood. (The Navigli were covered with walls when the first set of rings was built around Milan; if you look at a city map you'll see that the city is constructed in three concentric circles.) You can wander around here for an hour or two if you like colorful junk shops, secondhand shops, and the feeling of being in the real Italy. Cash only; no one speaks English.

## Ingròsso

The word *ingròsso* means wholesale in Italian. That's why we call this neighborhood Ingròsso; actually it's part of the Centrale train station area. This is a little area of shops, jobbers, and dealers who sell wholesale.

For the feel of Manhattan's Seventh Avenue, prowl down the Via San Gregorio, which crosses between the train station and the Piazza della Repubblica, and the side streets found there, between Via Luigi Settembrini and Via Vittor Pisani. Pisani is the main street, leading directly from the train station to all the hotels, so you probably are right there as you read this.

Ingròsso is not your top-of-the-line better dress wholesale neighborhood, true, but it's not unlike the garment center area of Manhattan— a junior and less expensive market area. Here you'll find a string of shops that may be marked *ingròsso* but will sell samples or pieces. A few shops even say "no samples sold" in signs in English. Saturdays in the summer are slow, but regular business hours during the week are fine, as are Saturdays during the fall and winter. Most of the designers are knockoff artists, but the goods are cheap, and if you have cash and can carry, you'll have a lot of fun. This is the kind of area we really recommend to mothers of teenage girls who want cheap fashion. We are not talking about quality.

This is throwaway chic or cheap thrills. Some prices may be high; keep your brains turned on at all times.

## Largo Augusto

The Jolly President is right here, and the Duomo can be seen right in front of the hotel, so you have that shopping area a long block away; but immediately on the square is the Via Durini, which you might miss if you didn't know you were looking for it. The Via Durini is a "downtown" shopping street near the Duomo and Corso Vittorio Emanuele, but it has blossomed lately, and as a result has many new stores, making it one of the most interesting streets in the area. It begins at the Jolly Hotel and ends at Piazza San Babila, only two blocks from Via Montenapoleone—rather convenient all around. Watch for Armani's temple of (somewhat) affordable chic, **EMPORIO,** as well as a few designer showrooms and cute little clothing places—and the shopping center Caffè Moda Durini, which houses teeny-tiny branches of a lot of big names and is the only resource for the less expensive Krizia Jeans line. You can snack downstairs in the Caffè Durini. Please note that you can catch a bus to **IL SALVAGENTE,** the discounter, at Largo Augusto or walk via the Corso Porta Vittoria (page 63).

## Zona Magenta

To prove that Milan is a city of many personalities, we take you to the Zona Magenta, a residential area where upper–middle-class people thrive. It's an older part of town, considered prime as an address. The main shopping street is called Corso Vercelli; it has branches of many Italian stores, from department stores (there's a good **STANDA**) to the usual **BENETTON.** There's an excellent **CROFF** for housewares.

You can walk the Corso Vercelli past the Piazzale Baracca, where it becomes the Corso Magenta, and all the way back to the Duomo. (Take the *metro* to Corso Vercelli; the red line runs under this stretch, so there are many stations if you give up on the walk.) Or consider the No. 29 streetcar.

The area is simply a nice middle-class area, but it's so nontouristy that you'll have fun pretending you are a native while browsing.

## Porta Vittoria

The Corso Porta Vittoria is such an important street in Milan that after it dead-ends into a traffic circle at a big monument it changes its name to Corso 22 Marzo. We won't even tell you what it changes its name to after that, because you'll be out of the heart of town.

The Corso Porta Vittoria begins shortly after the Duomo and leads out of town, in about the same direction that the yellow line of the *metro* will take if it is ever finished. Until the *metro* is finished, just use your feet. We particularly like this walk because you pass right by **IL SALVAGENTE,** the discount designer store.

The Vittoria part of this walk is an upper–middle-class neighborhood where you'll find branches of many favorite stores, such as **MAX MARA** and **BASSETTI.** This is where well-off locals shop, and it's very nontouristy—not unlike the Corso Vercelli but a little more scenic. There is a nice **COIN** department store. Then the street changes name to 22 Marzo, where you'll find a branch of **CROFF.** Shortly after Croff you turn left on Via Fratelli Bronzetti for Il Salvagente.

## Aprile

Way off the beaten track for tourists, where Romeo Gigli decided to open his first boutique, there is an up-and-coming neighborhood that doesn't have a lot to it as we go to press. However, the few retailers who have set up shop are inventive, creative, and exciting—so we expect more of the same to bloom. Between the Moscova and Garibaldi stops on the green line (Garibaldi is a train station) is Piazza XXV Aprile. After this plaza Corso Garibaldi changes its name and becomes Corso Como. **ROMEO GIGLI** is located off a courtyard on Corso Como; **HIGH TECH,** a huge furniture store featuring the kind of pieces you'd expect from a place with a name like this, is closer to the Piazza. Who knows what else is coming?

## The Big Names

**ALMA:** Founded right after World War II, the Alma Group packages their own designs, the work of young with-it designers, and a showcase environment in a snazzy-looking boutique. Alma sells about half their own designs and then the work of their "finds"—who usually turn out to become famous a few years after Alma showcases them. Among the Alma Group designers are Junko Koshino and Gianni Versace, who does a line called Spazio for Alma. The Mistèro line was created for rich teenagers.

**ALMA,** Via Sant' Andrea

▼

**GIORGIO ARMANI:** The Milan Armani boutique, the flagship store, is a temple to fine architecture and expensive furnishings. It's the kind of place you should walk into just to see. Unfortunately, the narrow door to the right side of the big picture windows is a little uninviting, and you may feel threatened if you know you aren't going to buy. Don't be scared.

Just sail right in. The help is friendly; they know the place is a sight for sore eyes and are appreciative of your compliments. All types of Armani items are sold here, for both sexes and for kids.

**GIORGIO ARMANI**, Via Sant' Andrea 9
**EMPORIO ARMANI**, Via Durini 24
**MANI**, Via Durini 23
**ARMANI KIDS**, Via Durini 27

▼

**BASSETTI:** A famous name in linens for years, Bassetti makes the kind of linens that fall between ready-to-wear and couture—but they're more affordable than the big-time expensive stuff and far nicer than anything you'd find at the low end. Although they do sell colors, their hot look is paisley fabrics in the Etro vein. There are branch stores in every major Italian city.

**BASSETTI**
  Corso Vercelli 25
  Corso Garibaldi 20
  Corso Vittorio Emanuele II 15

▼

**BENETTON:** What more can we say about Benetton and all their subsidiaries and divisions and success? Naturally, there are several Benettons in Milan, all over town. The one on the Via Montenapoleone is interesting, however, in that it appears to be much fancier than any other Benetton we've ever seen. It's much more elegant, more Old English or Ralph Laureny with a touch of marble thrown in, and it contrasts with the standard 012 shop a few doors away to the point of ridiculousness. Benetton prices traditionally are cheapest in Italy.

If you're looking for the best Benetton prices in Milan, veer off the main drag. You'll get better sales at any of the numerous Benettons on the Corso Buenos Aires, where real people shop, rather than the touristy stores on the Via Montenapoleone.

Excellent end-of-season sales; credit cards accepted; closed for lunch.

**BENETTON**, Via Montenapoleone 13
**012**, Via Montenapoleone 13

▼

**LAURA BIAGIOTTI:** Fans of Laura's won't see any reason to wait for Rome when they hit the Milan galleria, tucked into an ochre villa. Some people dream of spending the night in Bloomingdale's; our dream is to bring our sleeping bag to this shop. The selection is huge. The prices are, as always, high. If you want to make your own version, ask about the knitting yarns, which are also sold all over Milan in yarn shops.

**LAURA BIAGIOTTI**, Via Borgospesso 19

▼

**BOTTEGA VENETA:** Look, Bottega isn't cheap. But if you've got only $250 to your name, or at least to spend on this trip, the best thing you can do with it is buy a handbag on sale here. Be crazy and get a silly color. You'll be chic for life. We once hit an end-of-season sale where the merchandise was half price. The duty on leathergoods is 8%; don't be upset if you go over your U.S. Customs allowance. This is spending to save. The shop is small, not nearly as elegant as in Paris or even the United States, but who cares? Nonsale prices are better than in the United States, but not much. The average bag does cost about $500 when not on sale.

**BOTTEGA VENETA**, Via della Spiga 5

▼

**MARIELLA BURANI:** Exciting? You want exciting? You want to know why you just spent $600 (or more) on airfare to come to Milano? At last it is all revealed—this is what Italian design is all about. This is what the marriage of architecture and retailing is about. This is what theater is about. What about the clothes? you ask. The clothes are simple, outrageously expensive, rather similar to Armani. They are perfectly showcased in the very Italo-Japanese space.

**MARIELLA BURANI**, Via Montenapoleone 3

▼

**CACHAREL:** Although Jean Cacharel is a French designer, he has a magnificent shop in Milan that we think is his best showplace. Located almost next door to the Duomo, this modern shop has a demifirst floor and a huge downstairs. They stock men's, women's, and children's clothes as well as fragrance. We think this is one of the best resources for kids' clothing in the world, but it's all traditional. The end-of-season sales are legendary.

**CACHAREL**, Corso Vittorio Emanuele II

▼

**CHANEL:** This shop is a tribute to Coco's genius, Lagerfeld's grip on the line, and every woman's desire to be chic. This store is more fun than the one in Paris, but it's easier to get *détaxe* in Paris. Some Chanel is made in Italy. Prices are the same as in Paris, and not much lower than in the United States. Chanel scarves are discounted at the Rome airport.

**CHANEL**, Via Sant' Andrea 10a

▼

**ENRICO COVERI:** Coveri styles moderately expensive clothes in a somewhat trendy manner, and has the most incredibly stunning chain of international boutiques. Milan is the flagship, so be sure to look at this large shop one block from Montenapoleone.

**ENRICO COVERI**, Via San Pietro all' Orto 12

▼

**ETRO:** Etro has four shops in Milan, selling the traditional paisleys and paisley print leathergoods that have established the commercial fame of the company, as well as the men's and women's fragrances. The men's after-shave begins at $56 for the smallest size made. If the prices are too high simply browse around and pretend you're in a museum.

**ETRO**
  Via Montenapoleone 5
  Via Bigli 10
  Via Pontaccio 17
**ETRO** (Perfumes), Via Verri 5

▼

**FENDI:** The Fendi shop in Milan is small but well-stocked. Prices are so reasonable that one immediately wants to buy. If you are going on to Rome—wait! The stores in Rome are so incredible that you must experience them. One warning: If you are claustrophobic, the cram and jam of customers in Rome may make you feel a bit crazy. If so, buy in Milan, where there is no press. Although it's small, Milan Fendi is fun and shouldn't be shunned.

We were amazed at just how far $25 could go at Fendi. Prices appear to be the same in any Italian city. Any "Fendi" that says "elle" in little letters along the border is not the real thing.

**FENDI**, Via della Spiga 9

**FERRAGAMO:** Attention all Ferragamo freaks: The shoes aren't much less expensive here than at home. In fact, they're almost exactly the same price (within about $5). Now for some slightly better news: There are lines, styles, color combinations, and designs sold in Italy that aren't sold in the U.S., so that if you're looking for novelty or selection—then you'll have a ball.

There are fabulous sales at Ferragamo, of course, so all is not lost. And there is a branch store in every major city. The showplace is the Milan showroom, which is large, airy, and modern and contains clothes as well as shoes.

**FERRAGAMO**, Via Montenapoleone 3

▼

**GIANFRANCO FERRÉ:** Milan is his home and headquarters, so we do our buying (on sale, of course) in this sumptuous shop. Ferré is not cheap, even in Italy. Prices are 30% less than in the United States; sales are fabulous—but we're happy with our bargains at Il Salvagente. Go to the store just to breathe the rich air and fondle the well-constructed clothes.

**GIANFRANCO FERRÉ**, Via della Spiga 19

▼

**FRETTE:** As in most Italian cities, Frette has taken over in the same location where a Pratesi shop once stood. But don't panic; you can still buy Pratesi in their own new shops in Italy, in the U.S., or at the factory outlet outside of Florence.

Frette has two different lines, the everyday, rather average line which we don't find particularly special and an upscale line meant to compete with Pratesi.

**FRETTE**, Via Montenapoleone 21

**NAZARENO GABRIELLI:** A leathermaker who has branched out into ready-to-wear and everything else, Gabrielli produces a line that we categorize as Fendi meets Dooney & Bourke. You'll pay $150 for a linen and leather summer bucket bag, and $400 for a drop-dread chic leather bag. A smaller bucket bag comes in at around $330. Some of the leathers have a small imprint, but you won't find huge, tacky logos all over the merchandise.

**NAZARENO GABRIELLI**, Via Montenapoleone 23

▼

**GENNY:** Other than the fact that the doorway looks like the windows and we almost couldn't figure out how to get in, the Genny shop sells the Genny line in a high-tech, macho store, open through lunch. The architecture is as good as the clothes, if not better.

**GENNY**, Via Montenapoleone 8

▼

**ROMEO GIGLI:** Romeo, Romeo wherefore art thou? Designing up a storm of exciting but still wearable fashions for the woman who dresses to be noticed. His designs are often sold in boutiques and specialty stores (including Menswear at Kashiyama) rather than Gigli shops. The Gigli boutique (one of a few) is in the spare warehouse style, with clean white walls, high windows, a few pieces of modern furniture, and a few racks showing the clothes. Check out the multiple video screens in one section of the wall, but don't be distracted from the well-cut clothes. It's a statement, all right.

**ROMEO GIGLI at BIFFI**, Corso Genova 6
**KASHIYAMA**, Via Sant' Andrea 14
**ROMEO GIGLI BOUTIQUE**, Corso Como 10

**RICHARD GINORI:** The Richard Ginori store in Milan is large and fancy, with parquet floors and the atmosphere of a fancy china shop where you have to pay for anything you break—which you probably do. It has the haughtiest salespeople we've ever met. Ginori has a wide selection not only of their own designs but also of every major maker—Lalique, Baccarat, Aynsley, etc. Prices are outrageously high—you'll do much better at a U.S. discount source or at Reject China in London.

**RICHARD GINORI**, Corso Giacomo Matteotti 1

▼

**GUCCI:** There are several Guccis in Milan, all within a block of each other. The most confusing part is that one of the shops has two entrances with a large store in between them that makes you think these are two separate, small Guccis that may not even be very interesting. We're not privy to the latest in Milanese real-estate deals, but what's happened is that Gucci owns the underground rights to that middle store, so the two entrances are merely ways to bring you inside and then lead you downstairs to a very, very large showroom. If you like Gucci, now is the time to freak out. You will not see any crossover in merchandise at the shops, but do know that Gucci store policy is that a piece of merchandise can sit on the shelf for only one year—it must then be sent to the clearinghouse. One twitch of the eye will tell you how much merchandise is down there—everything from turquoise snakeskin handbags to Gucci double G gun holsters (honest).

The clothing shop, another piece of marble and chrome and money spent lavishly, is across the street from the leathergoods shop and up (or down, depending on which direction you're going) a hundred yards or so. If you're confused, ask.

**GUCCI**, Via Montenapoleone 2–5

▼

**KRIZIA:** We can't afford the top of the line here, but we pretend we can—just to be able to touch it. Our goal in life is to be the kind of woman who walks into this store and pays retail. Sometimes we can afford the Poi line, which is cheaper. Most of the merchandise is downstairs.

**KRIZIA**, Via della Spiga 23
**KRIZIA JEANS**, Caffè Moda Durini

▼

**BRUNO MAGLI:** Near the Duomo and a must if you love Magli; there's one shop for men and another one for women, with accessories and even some clothes. The selection is huge, and this is a *primo* Magli shop.

**BRUNO MAGLI**, Corso Vittorio Emanuele II

▼

**MISSONI:** We couldn't wait to get to Missoni in Milan, because we expected bargains galore. If this is your dream, forget it now. The Missoni shop is interesting, but the prices are high and the merchandise is not piled higher and deeper than anywhere else. You enter the shop through an obstacle course of a modern doorway that leads upstairs to a smallish loft housing the collection. Don't trip! This is modern Italian design at its finest.

**MISSONI**, Via Montenapoleone 1

▼

**MOSCHINO:** Fashion's bad boy has opened two shops in Milan to make up for the lost time when he had no shops of his own. His designs, especially the accessories and jewelry, are sold through other stores as well, but his shops give you insight into this man's wild and wacky sense of humor. Moschino's claim to fame has been creating fashion parodies, especially of Chanel designs, but his work has such flair that it becomes collectible on its own.

**MOSCHINO**
Via Sant' Andrea 12

▼

**NAJ OLEARI:** Bloomingdale's has discovered this Marimekko type of talent; universal fame cannot be far. Oleari is one of those total-look designers—you can buy fabrics, clothes, lunchboxes, tote bags, umbrellas—everything. It's particularly nice for kids. The newest addition to the ever-growing line: makeup.

**NAJ OLEARI**, Via Brera 5–8

▼

**PINEIDER:** Italy's most famous name in papergoods and old-fashioned, heavy-duty, richer-than-thou stationery is Pineider, with stores in every major city. The Milan shop is right near Piazza San Babila.

**PINEIDER**, Corso Europa and Piazza San Babila

▼

**PRATESI:** Pratesi linens are among the finest in the world. They claim that most of Europe's royalty was conceived between Pratesi sheets. Choose between solids or florals in bed linens, table linens, and bedclothes. Our terry bathrobes have lasted ten years.

This is a new store, opened as part of a whole new retail inspiration.

**PRATESI** (opening soon)

▼

**MILA SCHÖN:** One of the big names in Italian design, dating back from before World War II, the House of Schön has worked very hard at rejuvenating its image and offering wearable clothes for women under seventy. They've succeeded in creating something worth looking at, if you are used to looking at high-end ready-to-wear and couture.

**MILA SCHÖN**, Via Montenapoleone 2

▼

**LUCIANO SOPRANI:** For those in the know, Soprani is a good buy and an elegant name to drop. Soprani menswear is sold at Kashiyama. Soprani's secret line is the Gucci ready-to-wear. Soprani once designed the Basile line, which made him a local hero to the rag trade. He continues to work in linen, wool, silk, and the like to produce a couturelike casual look.

**LUCIANO SOPRANI**, Via Sant' Andrea 14

▼

**TRUSSARDI:** Clothes, ready-to-wear, sweaters, leathergoods, and then the usual leather and canvas-and-leather line. Trussardi is growing and expanding, all right. So are his prices.

Like most of the Italian design empires, Trussardi is a family enterprise. It's run by Nicolo Trussardi, who considers himself a designer-*cum*-businessman and is quite proud of the billion-*lire* business he built for himself and hopes to pass on to his children. His main job, he says, is to keep his firm moving ahead at a rapid pace in the design area to provide constant interest to the consumer and prevent fakes and rip-offs. He's certainly moving at a breathless pace.

**TRUSSARDI**, Via Sant' Andrea 5

▼

**VALENTINO:** Via Santo Spirito is a side street that has very little on it except Valentino. Why crowd the master, eh? Besides, it is quite a shop—or two. The men's store fronts on Montenapoleone. The flagship store in Rome is larger, but you can blow your money here. We've gotten VAT from these people! Sale prices can be affordable. Otherwise a piece of jewelry may be what you need. Prices begin at $100.

**VALENTINO**, Via Santo Spirito 3

▼

**ATELIER VERSACE:** Not to be confused with Gianni Versace's regular shop, this is a tiny couture space with clothes suitable for movie stars.

**ATELIER VERSACE**, Via Gesù 12

▼

**T&J VESTOR:** For the most part, we don't suggest to people that they buy sheets or towels in Europe, because these products are often better and cheaper in the U.S. However, when you get to T&J Vestor, it's another story—this is the house that acts as distributor for Missoni, and these Missoni sheets are something to behold. They are expensive—over $50 for a set—but they are unique and if money is no object when you worship at the altar of style, this is your kind of store. There are branches in almost all big Italian cities.

**T&J VESTOR**, Via Manzoni 38

# Department Stores

**LA RINASCENTE:** Check out the handbag department (vast) for a good selection of low prices on Mandarina Duck and other name brands. Other good departments are children's and active sportswear. The ski clothes are sensational. The men's floor also is good. We've never seen so many boxer shorts.

The big names are not well represented in women's fashion, but we have seen lots of "real people" clothes at excellent prices. If you need simple wool knits or jerseys for work, you can buy a worthy dress at a sound price. If you're looking for basics and don't care if you are wearing a name, check out the clothes here. Makeup is expensive.

**LA RINASCENTE,** Piazza del Duomo

▼

**COIN:** Pronounced "co-een," this is not as convenient or as much fun as La Rinascente, but if you're in town for a long time and want to check it out, there are four different locations. Coin specializes in designer-inspired looks—at moderate prices. The Corso Vercelli address is in the Zona Magenta. The Piazzale Loreta is at Buenos Aires. Piazza Giornate is in the Vittorio neighborhood.

**COIN**
Piazza Giornate 5
Corso Vercelli 30–32
Piazzale Cantore
Piazzale Loreta

▼

**STANDA:** Standa is like a nice version of K mart. Prices are quite reasonable.

**STANDA**, Corso Buenos Aires

▼

**UPIM:** This is your kind of store if you love K mart. The Corso Buenos Aires store is newer than the San Babila store, but both are clean and modern and filled with cheap fashion for all members of the family. And they don't close for lunch. So there. Buy your Carnival supplies here.

**UPIM**
   Corso Buenos Aires
   Piazza San Babila

## Shopping Centers

**CAFFÈ MODA DURINI:** Milan is a city of teen dreams, so it's no surprise that an entire shopping center of designer clothes and goodies geared to the teen and young twenties market should appear. Caffè Moda Durini is next door to the Jolly President, and is not to be confused with the Galleria. It's a high-tech kind of place with three levels to it and a bunch of small (like 500 square feet) boutiques; many are branch stores of big names. There is a Missoni here (very little stock), there is a Cacharel, there is even a Krizia Jeans store—which has the only Krizia merchandise we can afford in Italy. This is a good place to rendezvous with someone, to stop for coffee and a rest.

**CAFFÈ MODA DURINI**, Via Durini 24

▼

**GALLERIA VITTORIO EMANUELE:** The antithesis of Caffè Moda Durini, this is an old-fashioned European gallery that is one of the most famous addresses in Milan. Many modern shopping centers are based on this medieval example, which serves as the main meeting place for those visiting or living in Milan. Jammed with stores and cafés, the Galleria is also an architectural masterpiece. Don't miss Prada, Rizzoli, or the borders near the ceiling.

GALLERIA VITTORIO EMANUELE, Corso Vittorio Emanuele II

▼

**CENTRO COMMERCIALE BONALO:** If you have a yen to pretend you are a middle-class resident of Milan, if you've seen the hoity-toity world of Montenapoleone and decided that you want something you can afford, if you're game—or bored during lunch when everything else is closed—hop on the red *metro* line and get off at Bonalo, about fifteen minutes from the Duomo.

When you exit the station you'll discover you appear to be in the middle of nowhere. Follow the concrete path to the left, under the freeway and *voilà*—a shopping mall. Not much of a mall to a jaded American, but this is the big time to locals. What we like is the *hypermarché*. There are a few branches of well-known chain stores with middle- to lower-priced clothes and plenty of take-out places. A great place to spend an hour or two away from the mad rush.

CENTRO COMMERCIALE BONALO, Bonalo

# Menswear

**BOGGI:** Boggi specializes in the English look, the preppy look; whatever you call it, you'll find cableknit sweaters and plaid hunting trousers. There are several shops; the main store is near Via Montenapoleone. It's not cheap here, but the quality is very high.

**BOGGI**, Piazza San Babila 3

▼

**VALENTINO UOMO:** We've been known to wear these clothes ourselves, so we know them well. The knits are very sophisticated, the manufacturing is rather good, and the colors are always chic.

**VALENTINO UOMO**, Via Montenapoleone 20

▼

**VERRI UOMO:** Women can shop here, too, and soak up just the kind of ambience that money and good taste can buy. This is the Italian menswear look to a T. It's pricey, but who cares? If you go to only one hot new men's shop, this gets our vote. Spend $250 to look like $1,000,000.

**VERRI UOMO**, Via Pietro Verri at the corner of Montenapoleone

▼

**TINCATI:** Old-fashioned men's store or haberdashery (as they used to be called), with fine woods on the walls and an upper mezzanine filled with stock. Very good Old World reputation. Not for hotshots who want the Euro-Japanese look.

**TINCATI**, Piazza Oberdan 2

**CASHMERE COTTON AND SILK:** This is one of those fancy stores on the little side streets of Brera that is worth looking at, if only for its charm. Walk down a rather long corridor until you get into the store, which is modern with an old-fashioned feel. Milanese preppies (and yuppies) abound as they scurry to choose between the shirts, sweaters, and suits made only of the three fibers in the store's name. Prices are very, very high, but the shopping experience makes you feel like royalty.

**CASHMERE COTTON AND SILK,** Via Madonnina 19

▼

**ERMENEGILDO ZEGNA:** Zegna is a national hero of Italy—the family has excelled in the quality wool business for centuries. Until recently, the ready-to-wear was a small sideline. Now the world's richest men can buy the best suits that Italy ready-makes in a smattering of freestanding boutiques—there's one in Paris, one in Florence, and this shop in Milan, which is the closest to the mill in Biella and serves as the family flagship store. The shop is large and modern and sells classic tailoring to discriminating men. Although the house is famous for its wools, you can get other items—including cotton or silk dress shirts.

**ERMENEGILDO ZEGNA,** Via Pietro Verri 3

▼

**AB:** This is a very small shop, on a side street off of Via Vercelli, which has never seen a tourist in its life; but Bethany tells us it's a great source for reasonable prices on high-quality, English-style preppy clothes which are requisite for upscale northern Italians. The store is not much bigger than two closets (it has two chambers), and sells very traditional things like cableknit sweaters in high-quality fibers. The prices are very high; they just happen to be a little less than other big-name sources.

**A B**, Via A. Scarpa 9

▼

**EDDY MONETTI:** One of the leading sources for Anglo style in Milan, Monetti deals with rich gentlemen who want to look even richer. They handstitch suits and shirts but also sell off the rack, and will outfit him from head to toe. The Monetti customer likes special service and hates to shop—he wants to come here and be pampered and know that he'll walk out looking like a million—dollars, not *lire*. Some women's clothing.

**EDDY MONETTI**, Piazza San Babila 4

# Sporting Goods

**PETER SPORT:** Around the corner from the Duomo, Peter Sport is our backup or control group for sporting goods and active sportswear. We prefer to load up at Brigatti, but still we always check at Peter Sport. Peter Sport has three levels, a creaky elevator, and more stuff than you could ever dream of wearing, even if you are a professional athlete.

**PETER SPORT**, Piazza Liberty 8

▼

**BRIGATTI:** On the edge of the Golden Triangle, Brigatti is a giant of a store, with floor-to-ceiling wood paneling and stairways that lead up and cabinets that are higher than three men (they use huge ladders), and stock from here to tomorrow. All major brands plus a wide selection of no-names. Tons of Fila. You really do not need another sportswear listing in Milan.

**BRIGATTI**
Corso Venezia 15
Galleria Vittorio Emanuele

# Shoes and Leathergoods

Y ou could buy every pair of shoes in Italy and still want more. (At least, we could.) Shoe shops obviously abound. We try to stick to branded shoes in Milan because we'd rather have the quality we want to count on; we also like to buy names that are available in the United States, so that if we have a problem we can take them back or have them fixed. If you want no-name shoes, you will find them starting at $30 a pair. Better no-name shoes cost $50 a pair. But if the shoes make the man, then we vote for the big names:

**BELTRAMI:** Beltrami is a resource for those who love Maud Frizon, Walter Steiger, Andrea Pfister, etc. They do everything from traditional shoes and boots to the kind of glitz we heretofore thought only Maud Frizon was capable of. There are several shops in the central area around the Golden Triangle and the Duomo.

**BELTRAMI**, Piazza San Babila

▼

**SALVATORE FERRAGAMO:** The clothes are incredibly expensive and carried mostly in another very small shop, but the shoes here are well-made classics (they come in American sizes, by the way). The shop is modern, with all clean lines and white light and open space— all the better to see the shoes, my dear. Prices are not cheap, but you can get out of there with pumps for $135. Interesting fact: We took a pair of shoes we bought in New York there to be stretched and everyone was very nice and understanding of shopper's feet and couldn't be more helpful, but—get this—they had never seen that style before. The pump was made in a color that was not shown in Europe.

SALVATORE FERRAGAMO, Via Montenapoleone 3

▼

**MARIO VALENTINO:** More of the same shoes and leather clothes he's famous for, but the shop itself is quite strange—the seating area is in a circular sunken pit. Men's and women's shoes begin at $100 a pair. Elegant, expensive-looking; smells deliciously like expensive leather inside the store.

MARIO VALENTINO, Via Montenapoleone 10

▼

**DE BERNARDI:** Having nothing to do with leathergoods and everything to do with shoes, De Bernardi sells stockings, panty hose, and even underwear. Designer everything, like Ungaro panty hose and Valentino bras.

DE BERNARDI, Corso Vittorio Emanuele II

▼

**FRATELLI FIGINI:** At the corner of Piazza San Babila and Via Montenapoleone, Figini looks like a mini department store of shoes. It sells everything but is a major dealer for Andrea Pfister. If we could afford these shoes, we'd be happier people. The most incredible Pfister shoes in the world, all silver and lace and nonsense, cost $300. They would be more in the United States, but we don't spend that much on shoes. If you do, more power to you.

**FRATELLI FIGINI**, Piazza San Babila 3

▼

**LE TINI:** Maybe this means The Tiny, because this could be the smallest store we've ever been in. It holds a sofa, that's it. But it boasts a very long, skinny window where the real goods are displayed. There are mostly flats, and a few handbags—the shoes begin at $100 and remain moderately priced. The designs are very now, very current, very high-fashion, exactly what you want to buy when on a trip so you can show everyone at home that Italy has not lost its touch.

**LE TINI**, Via Montenapoleone 6A

▼

**L'ARCOLAIO:** If you are the kind of person who thinks nothing of spending $500 for a handbag, we have found a wonderful little shop off the Piazza San Babila where the quality isn't as good as Hermès, but they are trying. Most of the handbags are classic styles (they offer a version of the Kelley bag—$427—but it doesn't have a shoulder strap), with some evening bags in the flippier mode, à la Lacroix or Paloma Picasso. The store isn't large but is exactly the kind of find we can recommend with confidence.

**L'ARCOLAIO**, Corso Monforte 4

▼

**ALLA PELLE:** If you've spent time tracking down U.S. prices on well-made status handbags, you have probably been as shocked as we are at prices. We spent an entire day in New York looking for a Kelley-style bag and found the best we could do was $375. Here, in this tiny shop, we found the same bag with the same quality for under $200. The store is small, and not every single handbag is a winner . . . but about 80% of them are. Almost all the bags are over $100, so we're not talking dirt cheap. But for our money, this is one of the best hidden resources of Milan. The shop we visit is the Via Durini address, since that's in our main line of travel (almost next door to Armani), but the other addresses are easy to get to. They take all credit cards too.

ALLA PELLE
 Via Durini 27
 Corso Venezia 5
 Corso Porta Vittoria 38

▼

**POLLINI:** In an unofficial poll of shopping bags at the Pan Am counter in Milan, we discovered more American tourists with Pollini shopping bags than any others (and they weren't all with the same tour group). Pollini is an old-fashioned, traditional shoe shop selling top quality for excellent prices. Do not confuse it with Armando Pollini. Not necessarily the hot new fashions, but conservatives will love it here. There are about a dozen stores all over Italy, by the way.

POLLINI, Corso Vittorio Emanuele II 214

# Finds

**GALAXY:** Galaxy is a bread-and-butter specialty shop that sells designer ready-to-wear from French and Italian big names. You'll see a lot of fashion in one shop, here or at their second shop. It's across the street from Peter Sport and just one block from the Duomo.

**GALAXY**, Via San Paolo 1

▼

**GIO MORETTI:** There are three different Gio Moretti stores: one for men, one for women, and one—across the street—for children. You'll see all the big names here; for women, stock up on Sonia Rykiel, Complice, Genny, etc.

**GIO MORETTI**, Via della Spiga 4 and 6

▼

**FONTANA:** Modern Italian design of the most expensive and highest order. The interior is swank and very Milano, with marble and wood and counters that actually hang from wire from the middle of nowhere.

**FONTANA**, Via della Spiga 33

▼

**MICHELE MABELLE/MILANO MONAMOUR:** If that name isn't enough to make you fall in love, then the chain of stores is: Norma Kamali, Kansai, Thierry Mugler—all the fun stuff, with back floors and glitz all over and American rock 'n' roll and all those wild, sequiny

T-shirts you thought were so Roma (or Beverly Hills).

**MICHELE MABELLE/MILANO MONAMOUR,** Via della Spiga 36

▼

**SHARA PAGANO:** Glitz City for costume jewelry. Moderate prices, meaning earrings will start at $50—but this is the same stuff that costs $100 and up in the United States. It's not bargain basement, but we've bought many gifts here and think the quality is good. A big resource for fashion designers and editors.

**SHARA PAGANO,** Via della Spiga 7

▼

**NANNI STRADA:** Logan turned us on to this designer, who does a wrinkled version of the Fortuny pleat in natural fibers such as linen or silk. The garments are one-size-fits-all— and since they are already wrinkled as part of the design, they travel beautifully. Expensive, but so classic that they are worth it. Especially good for women with less-than-perfect figures.

**NANNI STRADA,** Via Gesù 4

▼

**MOLIGNONI & C.:** If you have bemoaned the fact that Milan is so sophisticated it's hard to find any country wares, you'll be delighted to find this pottery shop, which sells various *faenza* (faience) patterns in everything from plates and platters to jars, lamps, and small gifts. The selection is large, the location is good—only the hours are a little unusual. This store opens at 9 A.M. (few do) and closes at 1 P.M. for lunch, then doesn't reopen until 4 P.M., a little later than the norm. But it's worth planning your time around a visit. This is the best source in Milan that we've ever found for handpainted pottery.

**MOLIGNONI & C.**, Corso Porta Vittoria 47

▼

**PICOWA:** This store is where local brides register, and it has an excellent selection of kitchen gadgets and tableware. Concentrate on the unusual glass, pottery, china, tabletop, vases, and stuff. Forget the American patterns; it's the colored art glass that is *primo*.

Located in a gallery right off the Piazza San Babila and near many of the design showrooms, the store does not close for lunch, but is closed Monday mornings, like most stores in town.

**PICOWA**, Galleria Piazza San Babila 4d

▼

**ANTOINETTE:** If you love that magnificent, fancy handstitched Italian lingerie, you will need a straitjacket in this store. It's wildly expensive, but this is the most beautiful serious lingerie we have ever seen. This resource is so in that there is no need for a name on the door. You'll find just the letter A. And you know what that stands for.

If the address doesn't ring a bell, stay calm. This is only one block from Piazza San Babila and is across the street from Flos, the famous lighting designers.

**ANTOINETTE**, Porta Giordano 2 (Portici Monforte)

▼

**DANZA:** For exercise and dance buffs, this store (actually there are several branches around town) offers exciting looks that you won't find back home. Prices can be stiff, but you'll be the only one in your aerobics class in the outfit. There're dance and exercise togs for men, women, even children. This large store is at the end of Via Durini, therefore convenient to all.

**DANZA**, Corso Europa at Via Cavallotti

▼

**RAFFAELLA CURIEL:** This is couture in the new Milanese way: top-of-the-line ready-to-wear and accessories the likes of which are hard to find in the U.S. What's special about this designer is that she combines elements of the classic (Chanel) with a hint of the inventive ... but not too inventive. She is inspired by Lacroix and Lagerfeld without going overboard. Prices begin round $700.

**RAFFAELLA CURIEL**, Via Matteotti 14

# Gifts

**MORONIGOMMA:** This store has plastics from all over the world, so don't buy any of the expensive American products. Instead, get a load of the designer vinyl in the back, the car products, the household items, and the visual treat you cannot get back home. With its affordable prices, this may be the only store in Milan where you can go wild and not be sorry the next day. The store is conveniently located at the start of Via Montenapoleone, on the far side of the Piazza San Babila; there are many other wonderful design hangouts in the area. Alessi is across the street. This is a must-do if you are into design at all.

**MORONIGOMMA**, Via Braccio da Montone at Via Giusti

▼

**OFFICINA ALESSI:** Although you'll first see teapots in the window and more teapots everywhere inside, this really isn't a tea stop—it's design heaven. The shop—small upstairs, larger downstairs—carries work by every major architect/designer who ever cast a shadow, or a teapot: Michael Graves, Robert Venturi, Richard Sapper, etc. Check out the banister on the stairs leading down.

**OFFICINA ALESSI**, Corso Matteotti 9

▼

**CROFF:** The local version of The Pottery Barn, Croff has many branches around town and sells housewares and gift items, many of which are too heavy or too expensive to take seriously, even though this is the kind of store locals consider moderately priced. (We remind you that nothing in Italy is moderately priced.) Still, you may find some gift items here, or get some ideas on the latest Italian design trends or on household knickknacks. Worth doing for those who are into design.

**CROFF**
Corso Vercelli 10
Piazza Diaz (across from the Duomo)
Corso XXII Marzo 25 (near Il Salvagente)

▼

**IMMAGINAZIONE:** The Via Brera keeps to its reputation for offering the best of the hot and the new, the young and the kicky—this shop is crammed with weird but fun stuff including everything from plates and tableware to gift items and cuff links.

**IMMAGINAZIONE**, Via Brera 16

# Italian Design Hotshots

**CASSINA:** One of the long-standing big names in post–World War II design, Cassina makes mostly office furniture or show-off furniture—the kind of thing you buy because you are very avant-garde and want the world to know and your neighbors to whisper. The colors are bright, deep, and vibrant; the design lines are clean; and this large showroom is conveniently located, so you have no excuse not to drop by.

Arflex, a competing house (see next listing), is around the corner. Hit these two and you've got the makings of a museum tour.

**CASSINA,** Via Durini 16

▼

**ARFLEX:** One of the several big-name, big-time, hotshot design showrooms—Arflex has a lot of space and sprawl to display things like lipstick-red leather sofas and chairs with legs meant for dancing. Yes, they'll ship for you, although pricewise you may do better from an American distributor. Don't pass them by, however; browsing gives a good education in Italian style. The address is around the corner from the Armani shops and in the heart of the design district.

**ARFLEX,** Via Borgogna 2

▼

**SHED:** This large store has furniture and design from French big names as well as Italian and Japanese movers and shakers—all housed in a former cheese factory. A must-do for those with an eye for design, even with the understanding that you might not buy anything. Just seeing is a feast. Furthermore, the location is within walking distance of our favorite clothing discounter—Il Salvagente.

**SHED**, Viale Umbria 42

▼

**ALCHIMIA:** One of the longest-running shows in modern Italian design, Alchimia started it all and continues to be top-notch for seeing and believing. The very latest is always on display. Whether you buy or not, you can't be in Milan without getting part of your education from the master.

**ALCHIMIA**, Via Torino 68

▼

**ARREDAESSE:** Another of Milan's famous design showrooms, where modern furniture somehow becomes classical. Get a load of the purple leather sofa.

**ARREDAESSE**, Via Montenapoleone

▼

**GIORGETTI:** Here's a showroom full of upholstered modern furniture that actually looks comfortable. This is more like a movie star showroom than a hard-edged *Domus* magazine ad, but it's interesting nonetheless.

**GIORGETTI**, Via Montenapoleone at Santo Spirito

▼

**POLTRONA FRAU:** We just love the name of this furniture showroom and designer haven—it's so, well, German but the design is so, well, Italian. There's no question that this is one of the leading houses for leather-upholstered furniture that costs a fortune but will be considered collectible for the next century.

**POLTRONA FRAU**, Via Manzoni 20

▼

**MODERNARIATO:** Tired of bright red leather sofas? Had it with chrome from outer space? An important part of modern Italian design is the postmodernist look, and even some out and out Retro. Nostalgia isn't what it used to be: Now it's the hottest thing in Italian design.

This shop is just a doorway on the Corso Vittorio Emanuele II, and you must decide if you want to walk down all these endless steps or not. Do it, in the name of love! If you love gas pumps from the 1950s and American design from the fifties and sixties, you'll want to see just how well it works in Italy. This place is almost a museum, but everything is for sale. We're especially fond of all those old vacuum cleaners. Don't buy; do visit.

**MODERNARIATO**, Corso Vittorio Emanuele II

▼

**FLOS:** One of the most famous names in lighting, with a showroom that will knock your socks off. This is in the heart of the lighting district, so be sure to check out Artemide (Corso Monforte 19), across the street, and Arteluce (Via Borgogna 5), around the corner, while you're in the neighborhood.

**FLOS**, Corso Monforte 9

▼

**HIGH TECH:** High Tech is huge by Milan standards and rather large even to an American— an entire store selling the look we have come to associate with the city of Milan. Begun by

Aldo Cibic, formerly of Memphis Milano fame, the store is two stories high and crammed with furniture on the upper level. Take the *metro* to Moscova; do it now!

**HIGH TECH**, Piazza XXV Aprile 12

## Antiques in Milan

**M**ilan offers a wide variety of antiques, from French and Italian Art Nouveau and Art Deco (Liberty) to Russian and Chinese. Most of the shops are small and eclectic, many of them clustered together in typical trading areas or neighborhoods. Because the selection changes so often, it's hard to say which shops are best. We prefer just to wander on certain streets and see it all, touch it all, and pray that someday we can buy it all. Don't forget the Sunday fair in Bollate and the once-a-month Brera street fair. All of the following streets can be connected into one tour, by the way, if you merely work your way from the Golden Triangle to Brera.

Via Fiori Chiari: Not far from La Scala, off Via Solferino in the Brera district, is Via Fiori Chiari, loaded with tiny dealers. Browse and browse but don't miss **DECOMANIA** (No. 7) and **ROBERTA E BASTA** (No. 2)—both have incredible collections of Art Deco furniture, lamps, vases, and prints. There are many other important shops as well.

Via Gesù: Part of the Golden Triangle, Via Gesù hosts **GIANETTI** (No. 3), with its impressive selection of *haute époque* furniture.

Via Manzoni: Lots of things here to look at, but be sure to catch **FIUMI DARE AND FIO-LIO** (No. 39) for old timepieces, **MANZONI-FINARTE**

(No. 38) just to see the shop interior itself, and **DOTT. LUIGI MAGNETTI** (No. 45) for a wide, eclectic selection.

Via Montenapoleone: Home of the hoity-toity shops. Expect to pay top dollar in any one you may wander into. Don't miss the Russian icons at **MAZZOLENI** (No. 22).

Via Sant' Andrea: There're about ten shops within a short distance of each other. Try **PIVA** (No. 8), with its collection of rare majolica porcelains.

Via della Spiga: There're at least six shops here, and you'll love them all. **SUBERT** (No. 6) sells technical and medical instruments.

Corso Venezia: This very long street runs through the interior design district and serves many purposes. There are many antiques shops interspersed with the other shops (as in all these areas, of course). One of our favorites is **GALLERIA TOTO RUSSO** (No. 12), which specializes in Charles X to Louis XVI.

# Bargain Basements

**IL SALVAGENTE:** This is an operation that makes Loehmann's look classy. Walk through the gateway, down a driveway, and into a courtyard to enter. Don't be frightened—once inside, you'll feel a lot better. While the labels are still in the clothes, the merchandise is not organized well—so you must be feeling very strong to go through it all. There's so much here that you have a good chance of finding something worthwhile—but remember, you could strike out. But if you find your first treasure, strength will come rushing back to your body. Not everything is new; not everything is in perfect condition. On various visits, however, we did find a good bit of Krizia Poi, Gianni Versace, Valentino, Guy Laroche, Trussardi, et al.

Upstairs there are men's clothes, thousands of them—all yummy, but no large sizes.

You must check your handbag and packages in a locker; the atmosphere is drab; the display is zero. This place is for the strong, but we adore it. Hours: 10:30 A.M. to 12:30 P.M. and 3 P.M. to 7 P.M.; closed Monday morning and July 15 to August 30.

**IL SALVAGENTE,** Via Fratelli Bronzetti 16

▼

**MICHELA:** A resale shop where *Signore* and *Signora* may sell last season's clothes. Everything is secondhand, but we are talking major names, with the few piddling Benetton sweaters on the side racks. The convenient location makes it an easy quick stop for a tourist, although the staff prefers that you call ahead for an appointment. Many of the accessories were used only for photography or runway shows. Upstairs.

**MICHELA,** Corso Venezia 8

▼

**VESTI STOCK UNO** and **DUE:** These are two different shops owned by the same people; they are close to each other. It's almost impossible to get here on public transportation, so take a taxi and hope you get lucky. It's hard not to, with choices from Les Copains, Moschino, Versace, Montana, etc. Go to shop one first, then get directions and walk to shop two. There are men's, women's, and kids' clothes as well as accessories, so go and have a ball.

**VESTI STOCK UNO,** Viale Romagna 19
**VESTI STOCK DUE,** Via Ramazzini 11

**BALLOON:** Actually a business begun in Rome (see page 217), Balloon has a shop in Milan that does a big business in no-name basics, like cotton, silk, or cashmere sweaters. The goods are of high quality but cost less than at regular retail because they are made in China. To get to the shop, enter the lobby and walk straight ahead to the back, where you'll see a big door with the sign. You can take bus number 65 or trams 9, 24, 29, or 30. Ask at your hotel which line you are closest to.

**BALLOON**, Via Castelbarco 2

# Flea Markets

**NAVIGLI:** If flea markets are your kind of thing, work from the Porta Ticinese all the way to the Porta Génova and the Viale Papiniano on a Saturday morning. It's called the Mercato Papiniano, and is open 8 A.M. to 2 P.M.; things are most lively from ten o'clock to noon. You'll find the usual market fare—vegetables to Vuitton. Be sure to haggle. We've found new and used things here, as well as many items that were frauds or stolen goods. We love the knit-wear and the casual clothes—$10 for a sweater is our kind of deal. Who cares if it doesn't last forever? One of our favorite tricks: We buy solid-color sweaters as cheaply as possible, then buy appliqués at Minoti to sew on the sweaters. Don't do the sewing until you return to the States, because it will change the duty on the items! Great gift item; great throwaway fashion item.

**FIERA DI SENIGALLIA:** Every Saturday the locals flock to this fair to buy videotapes and tight blue jeans, hang out, and be seen. This market sells tons of junk, is very much for locals, and is only for the really bored or broke (in our book, anyway). Via Calatafimi, in the Navigli area.

**BRERA FAIR** (Mercatone dell' Antiquariato): Held once a month on the third Saturday of the month, this is considered the local biggie. About fifty antiques dealers set up stalls, and many artists and designers turn out. It is wonderful fun because everyone is dressed up and kisses everyone else on the cheek three times and does the social Italian bit while touching the goods sold from tables, flea-market style.

**BOLLATE:** Take the train or a taxi to this suburb of Milan, where there is a Sunday *mercato dell'usato*, or antiques market. Most of the dealers sell English antiques, if you can believe that; silver is especially hot, as are old prints. Not much in the way of bed linens, but some old hats, a fair amount of furniture, and lots of great, grand, wonderful junk. Very good Sunday entertainment. Consider renting a car for this day in the country.

# Milan on a Schedule

## Tour I: Best Buys to Bargains

With a whole day at your disposal, you can see the best of two worlds: Milan in its finest fashion, and Milan with its best buys.

1. Begin your day in the high-fashion district of Via Montenapoleone. Most of the major designers have boutiques in this area. The streets to walk are: Via Sant' Andrea, Via Gesù, Via Santo Spirito, Via Borgospesso, and Via della Spiga. Look at our listings under "The Big Names" (page 64) for the goodies you can expect to find, or just wan-

der and enjoy. About half of the stores on these streets are internationally known designer-related shops; the others are small but chic local treasures devoted to jewelry, antiques, children's clothes, or leathergoods. Many of the places we haven't listed are fun, so poke around here.

2. When finished with the Montenapoleone area, walk toward the Duomo on Corso Vittorio Emanuele II. Stop at Bruno Magli and La Rinascente (located right at Piazza del Duomo). Break for lunch now. (The shops will close, anyway.) It's a good walk from Point 1 to Point 2, so if you have a lot of packages, you may want to leave them somewhere or take a taxi to your hotel to unload and unwind.

3. Refreshed from lunch and maybe a nap, you're now ready for a few bargains. Grab a cab and go to our favorite spot, Il Salvagente (Via Fratelli Bronzetti 16). (This is near the Jolly President hotel, so you could take a bus or walk.) Pass between the iron gates (yes, you are in the right spot), and go into the courtyard and through the doorway to your left. Shop till you drop.

4. By this time you probably can't maneuver with all of your packages, so get a taxi back to your hotel, where it will take you another hour just to sort out all the wonderful purchases you have made. If you have the energy, walk back toward the Duomo on Corso Vittorio Emanuele II, which changes names several times but is a good shopping street for real people and gets you handily from Il Salvagente into town.

## Tour 2: "Real People" Walking Tour

There are two kinds of days we like to spend in Milan. The first is the high-fashion day outlined in Tour 1. The second is a day filled with fun shopping streets, some bargains, but mostly "real people."

1. Begin your day at Piazza del Duomo. Walk through the covered shopping mall toward La Scala (the Opera House). Proceed around Piazza della Scala to Via Verdi, which will connect to Via Brera. This is the artists' section of Milan and, as such, is full of fun little boutiques and galleries. On one of our trips we happened upon a small gallery selling ceramic Memphis Milano–style chairs. Don't ask how we got them home, but all our interior-designer friends loved them. Don't miss Via Monte di Pietà, as this is the location of Souleiado (1a). On Via Brera be sure to stop in at Laura Ashley (No. 4) and Naj Oleari (Nos. 5–8). Don't miss the back streets like Via Fiori Chiari, which are tiny and crammed with antiques and boutiques.

2. At this point take a taxi to Porta Venezia and walk up Corso Buenos Aires to its end at Piazzale Loreto. This is our favorite "real people" street because of the variety of good medium-priced merchandise. One warning: Do not attempt to shop on this street on Saturday if you can help it. The Italian working women all shop here on the weekend, and since most of the shopkeepers do not speak English, they will have no time or patience for you. During the week, the street is virtually empty, and you will be much happier. Some of our favorite shops on this street are Drugstore (No. 28), Lulu (No. 3), Mama Noel (No. 23), Buenos Sport (No. 4), and T&J Vestor (No. 52).

3. If you still have energy and are feeling very courageous, try the wholesale area, located in all of the streets directly off Via San Gregorio, which runs from Corso Buenos Aires to Via Vittor Pisani. You might have no luck, or you might have lots. There are

no designer clothes here, but it's nice for teens.

4. Walk from this Ingròsso area to the train station (Centrale), where there is also a bus terminal. Take a bus to Via Vercelli, where the rich "real people" live. There are branches of all the nice stores here. Stop at food stores to get a picnic to go.

5. Take your picnic to the Castello and enjoy.

## Tour 3: The Milanese Interior-Design Designer's Tour

Almost all of the interior-design showrooms are in the Golden Triangle and the chic Montenapoleone area bordered by Via Manzoni (Memphis Milano), Corso Venezia, and Corso Monforte (Flos). Here it is, guys—the latest in furniture, lighting, tabletop, and accessories. The showrooms range from the incredibly stimulating to the just so-so, but each one will capture your imagination. Please note that this tour does not include some biggies that are in different and not adjacent areas; you may want to catch them at a different time or with a taxi. Zeus: Clothes and furniture and accessories at a factory for hot talent (Via Vigevano 8); Castelli: It all began here (Piazza Castello 19); Museo Alchimia: Before Memphis there was Alchimia (Foro Buonaparte 55); High Tech: Definitely not Old English (Corso di Porta Ticinese 77); and Dilmos: Very interesting, very famous (Piazza San Marco 1).

Now for the tour:

1. Start with Memphis (Via Manzoni 46). Because there is no sign for the showroom, you will walk right by this building, which is at the end of Via Manzoni near Via della Spiga. Watch for the address, then walk

through the courtyard and up the stairs to the left. The Memphis showroom is on the first floor but is up two flights of stairs. Memphis is a good place to start because you've heard so much about it.

2. From Memphis walk down Via Manzoni and poke your head into Poltrona Frau (No. 20). This is one of the most well-respected and popular Italian leather sofa companies in Italy. Having a Poltrona Frau sofa is considered a sign of elegance and good taste on your part. Congratulations.

3. Next door is Selvini (No. 45). Here's where you find the modern furniture in chrome.

4. Lisio (No. 41a) sells magnificent brocaded silks and damasks of the old, classic school.

5. Now turn down Via Montenapoleone and stop at Sormani (No. 26). Don't let the small display space deter you. Upstairs there are two floors of Sormani designs that will knock your eyes out.

6. Across the street (at No. 27e) is Saporitta Italia, which manufactures designer pieces, has made a name working with the Missonis, and did the Missoni showroom.

7. Move on to Techno (No. 27c), which has three floors of office furniture, much of which will work in your home—if your home is not Country French.

8. Make sure you stop at Knoll (No. 11), the founders of the office-at-home look, and Venini (No. 9), a famous glass showroom.

9. At the end of Montenapoleone, turn left on Corso Venezia and go across the street to De Padova (Corso Venezia 14). De Padova has some wonderful renditions of American Shaker furniture, believe it or not, as well as exciting pieces from a whole group of

international designers. Don't miss any of the several floors.

10. Now walk down Corso Venezia to Piazza San Babila and take a left on Corso Monforte. Flos (Corso Monforte 9) is the lighting expert you've been reading about in the design publications. Then there's Artemide (No. 19), Arteluce (Via Borgogna 5), and Arflex (Via Borgogna 2).

11. From Via Borgogna connect to Via Durini, which bisects it at an angle; try your map if you get confused here. (We were lost for an hour.) Via Durini has several small showrooms—Lydia Levi Point (No. 17), Busnelli (No. 21), and Simon (No. 25). But the real reason to come here is the Cassina showroom (No. 18), which is the most spectacular showroom and design collection in all Milan.

# Day Trips

While Milan is a rather colorless, industrial town that lacks the *joie de vivre* we love in other European cities, the countryside is lovely. Once you get past the immediate industrial area and move into the hills and forests, you'll see a part of Italy you'll never forget. Nor will you soon forget the bargains to be had out here in the hinterlands. Many of the big-name designers have their factories within an hour's drive of Milan—the job is to decide which one you want to hit or which direction you should fan out to. We always suggest to our friends that they go on a driving trip for the fun of it and plan to stop at just one or two factories to see what's cooking. We've had so many different experiences at different factories that we do not promise you with all certainty that you'll get the deal of the century. We've marked our listings accordingly. *Note:* We have found that every factory we've called from Milan to see if we could come shopping said *no,* but when we showed up they said *si.*

Our favorite location is the Lake Como area, where you get the jet-set shops, the resort atmosphere, and all the fabric factories that make life so plush. If you're planning on one side trip, this is the one to take. If you have a car and are looking for adventure, try some of the other little cities and factory outlets we have listed here. Expect nothing and you won't be disappointed.

If you are not up to driving a rental car, you may want to splurge on a car and driver. You will break even in terms of what you save by shopping in such remote areas, and you'll probably have a lot of fun. It costs about $250 for a day (that's without tip), and solves many of your problems—the driver will speak English and Italian, the driver will know where he's going, the driver will help you haggle on prices when deemed appropriate, the driver will help you negotiate lunch, the driver will guard your packages in the car while you are free to shop at each stop. The driver will never look at his watch and say, "Hon-eeeee, can you move it along a little, pleeeeease?" Ask your concierge about getting a car and driver. We use Autonoleggio Pini, telex 322043 Pini I. They are associated with an international company (Carey) that has sliding rates depending on what city you are in. (Milan happens to be one of the cheaper cities.) If possible, book your driver ahead of time during the tourist season, because it is harder to get a car and driver then.

## Lake Como Area

The town of Como is the center of the silk industry. It's at the southern end of Lake Como, about fifty kilometers north of Milan. The town caters to the wealthy landowners who live in villas surrounding the lake. Nearby is Villa d'Este, another jet-set resort, approximately fifteen minutes farther to the north.

If you're on a tight budget, you'll probably adore driving around the Como area—hotels, food, and wine are cheaper than in Milan, and shopping bargains abound at every doorway. Don't expect anyone to speak English, but if your Italian is passable or you're a good sport, you will have the adventure of your trip. (If it's too much adventure for you, go with a car whose driver speaks Italian and English.) Best buys in the village shops are in clothes and leathergoods. While you'll find lots of antiques, most of them are fakes. But if you love it and the price is right, who cares? Remember that U.S. Customs wants an item to be 100 years old or older for you to bring it in without duty.

If you love fabrics, you owe yourself a visit to **SETERIE MORETTI**, Via Garibaldi 69, in the town of Como and right on the main square, on the corner of Via Galio and Via Garibaldi. Seterie Moretti distributes signed fabrics to retail sources, such as Galtrucco in Milan and Liberty in London. They retain the screens and rerun them without the designer name and with a slight variation in design. As a result you get fabrics that look familiar but at the same time are slightly different. There are five rooms of fabrics at Moretti; they speak English and accept credit cards. If you leave Como on the Lugano road going northwest and turn onto SS 340 to begin the drive around the lake, you will get to **RATTI**. Go with a driver or someone from the town, because the factory and its shop are on the estate of an old villa that is not visible from the road. Go up the private driveway, to a gate where a guard is stationed. You will have no trouble getting in, although having an Italian-speaking driver will make you feel less tense. No one here speaks English; having the driver or a guide is a morale-builder.

Once inside the villa, we were sent through the garden to a room that was packed with designer scarves. Every French and Italian designer we could imagine was represented (no Americans). We bought scarves from Valentino, Givenchy, Céline, and Dior. There were others that interested us, but we were told they were not for sale yet. Each large-size scarf (the size of a shawl, not a tiny babushka) cost $25.

There were also men's silk bathrobes for sale ($90) and bolts of silk from which fabric is sold by the meter.

There are two international fabric fairs outside Milan: Ideacomo, which is held at Villa d'Este, and Ideabella, held twice a year at Hôtel des Îles Borromées in Stresa. These are trade events, so don't expect to bop in and buy three meters of the same linen they just sold to Yves Saint Laurent. But if you love fabric and fashion, this is the place to see it all.

# Parabiago

Parabiago is an industrial suburb of Milan, where many of the shoe factories and leather-accessories people have offices. There is no public transportation. You can rent a car and go outlet shopping, remembering that even factory stores are closed at lunch.

**STEFANO SERAPIAN:** The star of the trip to Parabiago is the Stefano Serapian factory.

Serapian is sold in the United States and is much like Mandarina Duck—rubberized handbags and luggage with the Italian high-tech look. The store next to the factory is set up for tourists, but most of the clientele is Italian. Besides the rubberized look, there are skin handbags and even some clothes. There's a lot to see and buy here; the quality seems as high as at Moskowitz (a famous U.S. maker). We believe that the factory may work for some of the bigger names, such as Bally. It's worth the trip.

**STEFANO SERAPIAN**, Via Jommelli 35–37, Parabiago

▼

**FRATELLI ROSSETTI FACTORY:** There is a Fratelli Rossetti boutique in Milan (at Via Montenapoleone 1), but why shop there when you can go to the factory in Parabiago? The Rossetti factory has no ads and no markings—it kind of looks like a prison from the outside. The factory shop is in a separate building from the factory, and houses a large selection of men's and women's shoes and boots. It is a big open room with blue rubber flooring. The shoes are displayed on L-shaped tables. The help does not speak English but is very friendly. Men's shoes in traditional styles cost $45 a pair; more elaborate slip-ons cost $75; boots range from $50 to $80; high-heel pumps begin at $60. Hours: 8:30 A.M. to noon and 3 to 6 P.M., Tuesday to Saturday; closed Monday morning.

**FRATELLI ROSSETTI FACTORY**, Via Cantu 24, Parabiago

▼

**CLAUDIO MORLACCHI:** While you're in Parabiago, stop by Claudio Morlacchi, where we've always had great good luck. The factory looks like a house, but don't be alarmed. Push the large wooden door and enter into a light, airy courtyard. To the right is a room with a small but wonderful display of all the shoes the Morlacchi people make. Among Morlacchi's clients are Lanvin and Guy Laroche. Hours: 9 A.M. to noon and 2:30 P.M. to 7 P.M., Monday to Friday. Closed Saturday.

**CLAUDIO MORLACCHI**, Via Castelnuovo 24, Parabiago

# 6 ▾ VENICE (VENEZIA)

## Welcome to Venice

**W**ater, water everywhere, but plenty of room to shop—that's why we love Venice. Actually, this city is a group of over a hundred islands connected by four hundred bridges—and each one leads to a shop, a church, or a pizza parlor. What more could anyone ask? Founded in A.D. 451 by survivors of the Roman Empire, Venice provided a cultural and political link between Eastern and Western civilizations for many centuries and became a leading and wealthy trading port in the 13th century. People have been shopping there ever since.

The absence of cars allows leisurely browsing of the shops, churches, *piazzas,* and palaces. Every area contains boutiques stocked with the silver, lace, fine glass, papergoods, and leather items for which Venice has become famous. The most essential thing about shopping in Venice is that you are forced to walk just about everywhere, so even if you are just a museum person, you go by the shops and can look in the windows. Conversely, even the most dedicated shopper is still going to get an extra surge of excitement just from walking by the churches and museums. In Venice, culture and clutter, of the retailing sort, are all tied into one very attractive bundle.

You will find that most shopkeepers speak English and are quite used to a ton of tourists. All shops are anxious for business. If you are in Venice in winter, beware! The fog comes in around three o'clock and gives everything a mystical, almost fairyland atmosphere but makes it very hard to find the bargain you are so avidly hunting. If you happen to be in one of the side alleys off a main street, it is easy to get confused as to which way you should be going. Worse yet, if you are on the *vaporetto* (water bus), you can't see the shops at all! However, the shops are virtually empty, and the shopping is divine. (Winter also is the time to get the room of your choice at any of the several palace hotels.) In the summer the shopping is hectic and crowded, and although the same wonderful stores are there, you might not see them through all the people!

Everywhere you look in Venice, you will discover another "find." We have given you some of our favorites; doubtless you'll find your own as you wander. Don't be afraid to go down a small street and look in the smallest of windows. In the last few years retailers have gotten into New Wave architecture. For the first time in centuries there is new pizzazz in old buildings. Don't miss the Coin Rialto store, which was just rebuilt.

# Booking Venice/1

There are more and more books being published on Venice all the time, so you'll have no trouble finding traditional guides, special guides, or nonfiction works. There are no local shopping books published, although the hotel freebie *Un Ospite a Venezia* has ads and maps and visitor information.

There's also *A Key to Venice,* published by Hoepli and written in English. At a pricey $20, it does tell you everything you need to know about Venice and the Veneto.

## Booking Venice/2

Needless to say, it's often hard to get hotel space in Venice, because everyone wants to visit the original Disneyland city. We know many who escape the summer crowds by staying at the beach hotels at the Lido. Others stay in Mestre. Our favorite trick, especially during Carnival or high season—come in as a day trip. Venice is just a three-hour train ride from Milan. For something like Carnival, where you want to be part of the action and then you want to get out as fast as you can before you have a screaming breakdown (some 250,000 people jam San Marco each day on the Carnival weekends!) this is an ideal ploy. But if you've come to stay, then just about any hotel will do. Some just happen to be a little more magical than others:

**HOTEL DANIELI:** Because it is so easy to get lost in Venice, we try to stay at the same hotels all the time. The Danieli is the perfect shopper's hotel, because it's right on the edge of San Marco and even has its own gondola stop, San Zaccaria. Location and elegance, with summertime street vendors at the front door. Who could ask for anything more? Expensive.

HOTEL DANIELI, Riva degli Schiavoni 4196

▼

**HOTEL EUROPA E REGINA:** Not quite as grand as the Danieli, but more old-fashioned European and right smack on the Grand Canal. Old-fashioned charm galore. Your landing stop for the gondola is actually San Marco. Expensive.

HOTEL EUROPA E REGINA, San Marco 2159

# Getting There

Although it is possible to fly to a nearby airport, we come by train, and we have one important tip: There are two stations for Venice, but one of them is not in Venice. If you are staying in Mestre, which many people do in order to get a cheaper hotel room, you want to get off at Mestre. If you are staying in Venice, don't believe anyone who tells you how easy it is to train to Mestre and then make your way into Venice. You want a through connection that goes to the station in Venice—Santa Lucia—and that's all there is to it.

During peak seasons (summer and Carnival), consider getting to Venice from Milan—it's a three-hour train ride on the *ràpido*.

# Getting Around

From the train or the bus station you have many choices of water transportation. A water taxi is going to be very expensive; we suggest a water bus. The "bus" stops at several set landing stops, all of which are near something you want to see. You'll also want to do a lot of walking. And getting lost. The best part about being in Venice is what you can find when you get lost.

## Lost in Venice

Although we have many store listings in Venice and most have numbered addresses, you probably will not find the shop address too useful. The best way to shop Venice is by neighborhood and by wandering around. There are signs at almost every turn that point to *Rialto* or *San Marco* (usually these are in opposite directions). If you are tempted to look all around before you buy anything, do make sure you know your way back to a certain store, should you want to return.

## Prices in Venice

Italians will tell you to never buy anything in Venice because the prices are hiked up for tourists. As tourists who happen to shop a lot, we have found some items in Venice to be good buys. There are some things you don't want to buy anywhere else anyway (like masks), and while you can wait on marbleized paper until you get to Florence, if you see something you love and can afford, there's really no reason to hold back. Paperweights (many of which aren't even made in Venice, but are flown in from Eastern bloc countries, where they are cheaper) cost about the same in Venice as they do in other Italian cities as well as in the United States—unless you are talking about a serious collector's item. Many of the most charming things we've seen in Venice have been handcrafted items sold under tents or from booths during Carnival. No matter what the price, you can't duplicate these goods in another city or at another time, because they carry with them all the memories of the day. Overpaying for a souvenir is one of the privileges of attending Carnival, or of just being in Venice.

## Hours

**H**igh season is March to October, and shops are open from 9 A.M. until 12:30 or 1 P.M. and then reopen at about 3 or 3:30 P.M. until 7:30 P.M. If lunchtime closings bore you, remember that the shops on the nearby island of Murano do not close for lunch! Off-season, shops are closed on Sunday, and on Monday until 3 P.M. In season, some shops actually are open on Sunday afternoon. Check with your concierge for exact opening and closing times when you are there. Beware of holidays, saint's days, etc.

The street vendors, who work mostly in summer, stay open until the light begins to fade, which in the height of summer can be quite late. We've seen the pushcart vendors in front of the Hotel Danieli (this is a favorite pushcart hangout, by the way, which probably is why we like this hotel so much) begin to close down at 9:00 P.M. in high season. And while we're on the subject, those pearls are made out of glass; they're not cultured.

## Neighborhoods

**T**echnically, every stop on the water bus in Venice offers a different neighborhood. Not all of them are touristy, either. We always seem to marvel that "real people" do live in Venice, but if you ride around in a water bus long enough, you'll see that some parts of Venice are very normal—they're just awfully close to water. We are not going to give you a blow-by-blow of each stop, but most of our neighborhoods are trading areas that come to be named after water bus stops.

*Note:* Most of the shops are found in the historical and artistic center, between the Rialto Bridge and Piazza San Marco. Looking at a map can be very confusing because of the cobweb of interconnecting streets, bridges, and canals. Finding an address can be equally difficult, as many streets and shops show no numbers, or the numbers are clear but the street they are on is not clear. You can have a great time in Venice without the use of any map or any guidebook—merely by getting lost and getting found. If you want to use your time wisely, or find something specific, you will need help. We've even been known to hire a guide if we are in town for only a day or two. Getting lost and getting found has its charm, but it can be very frustrating.

## Merceria

One main street will carry you from Piazza San Marco to the Rialto Bridge—Merceria. It hosts hundreds of shops. Many of the shopping streets we mention branch off this one thoroughfare, or are very close.

Merceria is not a water bus stop (San Marco is), but if you'll get yourself to Piazza San Marco and stand at the clock tower with your back to the water, Merceria will be the little street jutting off the arcade right in front of you. If you still can't find it, walk into any shop and ask. You need not speak Italian.

# Venice

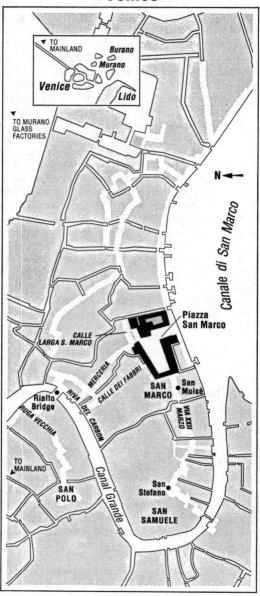

## Piazza San Marco

This is a very specific trading area—the four rows of arcades that frame Piazza San Marco. Three of them create a U shape around the square; the fourth is at a right angle to one of the ends of the U. There are easily a hundred shops here; a few of these shops are showrooms for glass firms, and a few sell touristy knickknacks, but most are jewelry shops (or cafés). Although many of these shops have been in business for years and some of them have extremely famous names, this is not our favorite part of Venice for shopping. We tend to ignore all these shops in one big lump, even though that is grossly unfair.

## Beside San Marco/Behind San Marco

Now, here's the tricky part. "Behind San Marco" is our name for the area that includes San Moisè and Giglio and is best represented by the big-time shopping drag called Via XXII Marzo. This street comes off of Piazza San Marco from behind and forms an L with the square and Merceria.

If you read an address of a shop that has a number and the words "San Marco" after it, and if it is in this book, it probably is on the Largo San Marco, in the neighborhood we call "Beside San Marco." We list very few stores that actually are on the Piazza San Marco. But many of our listings are "behind" or "beside."

## Giglio

Giglio is just a little square that suddenly appears, and it means little to you except that this is the main antiques area of Venice. Unless a shop is actually on the *piazza,* it probably will have a San Moisè address, so you may get confused. But then, Venice is just like Tokyo—it's impossible to talk about an address without getting confused.

## San Samuele

A water bus stop, San Samuele is a "real people" part of town that you might not think of on your own. It is pretty far to the back of the "Behind San Marco" shopping area, although it certainly is within walking distance and isn't that far from Giglio. San Samuele is the area where the up-and-coming artists and artisans have their shops and galleries. This is where the hot new talent goes because they can't afford higher rents or stand the commercial pressures of other locations. It is very secluded and special and charming. San Samuele leads to San Stefano, which is also an up-and-coming area one *piazza* over on the way back to Giglio. One of our favorite tours of Venice is to take the water bus (we get on at Zaccaria, which is the stop directly in front of the Danieli) to San Samuele and walk back to the Danieli. The streets are well-marked; just keep choosing the ones that say *San Marco,* and eventually you will get there.

## Rialto Bridge

They might just as well have named it the Retailo Bridge—not only are there pushcarts and vendors in the walkway before the bridge, but also there are shops going all the way up and down the bridge. The stores are not the crumbling, old, charming shops that line the Ponte Vecchio in Florence—there're teeny-bopper shops, leathergoods stores, and even sporting goods stores. We're shocked that despite the huge number of street vendors from San Marco to San Zaccaria, there are street vendors here *who are selling things we've never seen before.* Most of it is extremely touristy junk. But we look, anyway.

## Over the Bridge

Once across the Rialto, you'll hit a two-pronged trading area. In the arcades behind the street vendors—to the left—there are established shops; in the streets and to your right are greengrocers, food vendors, cheese stalls, and, in summer, little men selling little pieces of melon. You can have a walking feast for lunch in any season. Once over the bridge and past the immediate arcades, you bear left and follow the shops and crowds toward San Polo. No, this is not a tribute to Ralph Lauren. The shops here are a little more of the "real people" nature and a little less expensive. On the other hand, a large number of them are smaller branches of the big designer shops on the big island.

## Piazzale Roma

This is by no means a hot retailing area, but it is where the bus station is and where you will get your *vaporetto* if you come in from the airport, or if you come by bus. (The train station is not here.) Where there're tourists, there're shops. In the case of Venice, or Venice in summer, where there're tourists, there're street vendors—scads of pushcarts selling everything from T-shirts like the one worn by your favorite gondolier to plates of the Doge's Palace.

## Murano

Known for its glass factories, Murano is a monument to the ambivalence of the sophisticated traveler. It's our idea of heaven *and* hell to spend two hours on Murano. We have no mixed feelings about getting there—it's easy and it's inexpensive and it's fun. Even your kids will enjoy the ride. Get the No. 5 at San Zaccaria, in front of the Danieli. It costs the same amount of money to go to San Samuele as it does to Murano, which hardly seems fair. Murano is what we called a "field trip" in the third grade. It can be combined with a trip to Burano (take the No. 12), or you can turn around and come back home. Murano is the perfect lunchtime adventure. Do not bring small children or strollers with you.

When you get off the boat at Murano, you'll know you're there when you see the giant signs that say *fornace* (furnace); you have two choices—really to work the area, or to realize quickly that this is one of the biggest tourist traps known to mankind. By the way, you can get a free boat ride—private boat, even—if you go to Murano with a hawker. He gets 30% of what you spend in a secret kickback scam, and you get a lot of pressure to buy. We are not at all amused by the whole scene and like to pay for our own boat ride, thank you very much, and to go only to the showrooms that feature New Italian style. If you like the staid stuff and want to overpay for it, you're on your own. For New Italian style, see:

**BAROVIER & TOSO:** Very trendy showroom with the latest designs in hot colors and sophisticated styles. They will ship for you at moderate prices—but expect to pay several hundred dollars for a vase. This is serious art, folks, so if you're looking for cheap gifts to send home, forget it.

**SENT:** A double showroom with jewelry and home furnishings items; very modern and very chic, not as wild as some of the others.

**FOSCARINI:** This is a real showroom for important lighting fixtures that look like they're imported from outer space.

**LA FILIGRANA:** Another showroom, but this one is more equipped to sell to individuals rather than designers. This is where you get the two-foot-wide red glass platter for the head of Señor García.

**VENINI:** Showroom to the trade only, by appointment. Drat.

If you want outstanding paperweights or decent gift items, try:

**DOMUS VETRI D'ARTE:** Part retail, part showroom. You can get a 20% discount here if you buy in bulk. Carlo Moretti's work is featured here, as is the work of many famous glass designers. The selection of paperweights also is vast. Paperweights cost from $15 to $35, depending on size and style. At these prices, the paperweights are not signed and are not considered works of art by U.S. Customs. (A signed paperweight is considered a work of art.)

## Burano

Although Murano and Burano sound like twin cities, they are not. But if you visit the two in the same afternoon (you can get the water bus from Murano to Burano) you can sightsee and do some shopping at the same time. As touristy and crass as Murano is, Burano is natural and homespun. That's just what it is, since the fishermen and their wives have been making lace for centuries. Naturally, the lace you came here to buy is handmade. Therefore it is expensive—a fine tablecloth will cost in the tens of thousands of dollars. In fact, linen sheets with lace borders cost thousands of dollars. Go see, touch, smell. You'll love it.

# Specialty Stores

S hopping in Venice is easy if you love big-name designers. The really big names (such as Gucci) have their own shops, but there is much more of a tendency in this community for the designers to sell to small, trendy boutiques that carry several names, rather than for there to be rows of individual boutiques for each designer on his or her own. These are the biggies, boutiquewise:

**ARBOR:** Several boutiques, on the big island as well as at the Lido beach—Arbor carries the hot names, such as Byblos and Genny. The men's shop is one of the best we've seen anywhere for that stylish Italian look that thin men love to wear.

**ARBOR**
San Marco 4759
Gran Viale Lido 10a

▼

**ELYSÉE** and **ELYSÉE 2:** This is not one, but two very sleek boutiques carrying Mani, Maud Frizon, Mario Valentino, and the Giorgio Armani ready-to-wear collection for men and women. Armani is here exclusively. This also is a good place to check out the cheaper versions of Valentino—those licensed by GFT. Each shop has its own selection, including some shoes.

**ELYSÉE**, Frezzeria 1693, San Marco
**ELYSÉE 2**, Calle Goldoni 4485

▼

**DRAGANCZUK:** The most expensive Ungaro ready-to-wear we've ever seen, but a lovely shop. You can get a discount through the CIGA Shopping Card. We need more help than 10% to shop here, but it's fun to look. Very swank.

**DRAGANCZUK**, San Marco 2288

▼

**LA COUPOLE:** Once again, two boutiques carrying the same big names, and many lines. Both shops are small and elegant; prices are high. Our favorite one is near Harry's Bar and carries Kenzo, Rocco Barocco, Enrico Coveri, Loretta Di Lorenzo (for women), and Venturi (for men).

**LA COUPOLE**
  Via XXII Marzo 2366
  Frezzeria 1674, San Marco

▼

**V & V:** Not far from Harry's Bar, this is a small specialty shop that carries all the big names you love to wear.

**V & V**, Frezzeria 1233, San Marco

# The Big Names

**BENETTON:** There are so many Benettons in Venice that you don't know if you are lost and seeing the same shop over and over, or have come to yet another one. Benettons are everywhere. We think there are three of them, not counting the Stefanel. There's also the children's shop, 012, at yet another location, San Marco 1489.

**BENETTON**, San Marco 260

**BOTTEGA VENETA:** For all you Bottega lovers, this is a must-see. Don't let this tiny little shop fool you. There's a remarkable selection of all your favorite Bottega styles and colors, and when you finish spending your life savings, you can go around the corner to Harry's Bar for a drink. Medium-sized woven tote bag, $330. Sales are better in Milan.

**BOTTEGA VENETA**, Calle Vallaresso 1337

▼

**FENDI:** If you're not going on to Rome, blow your wad here. Otherwise, just pick up a few gift items so you still can do some shopping in Rome (unless, of course, you must purchase a suitcase immediately to haul all your new bargains). This large shop is quite well-stocked, with all of the famous Fendi styles.

We find it marvelously amusing (not to mention convenient) that there is an American Express instant cash machine just two doors away from Fendi.

**FENDI**, Salizzada San Moisè 147

▼

**GUCCI:** The same old stuff. Accessories are moderately priced, but ready-to-wear is expensive. The luggage is not that outrageously priced—you can get a nice, large Gucci suitcase for $250; briefcases begin at $50.

**GUCCI**, San Marco 258

▼

**JESURUM:** Located in a 12th-century church since 1868, Jesurum has upheld and continued the tradition of Venetian lacemaking, which was all but lost in the early 1800s. Just before the art would have died out, two Venetians undertook to restore it. One of the two was

Michelangelo Jesurum, who along with restoring the industry and putting hundreds of lace-makers to work, also started a school so the art would not die.

When you enter the Jesurum lace factory and showrooms, be prepared to flip your wig. The old church has been left with all its beautiful inlaid arches and its vaulted ceiling. Beautiful lace and appliquéd table linens and place mats are displayed on tables throughout the room. Intermingled with the table linens is a line of sportswear that is vividly colorful. The sportswear and beachwear sell well, but the real attraction of Jesurum still is its lace.

**JESURUM**, Ponte Canonica, San Marco

▼

**KRIZIA:** Stocked much like the Milan shop, this place is great—if you can afford it.

**KRIZIA**, Calle delle Ostreghe 2359, San Marco

▼

**BRUNO MAGLI:** Almost set into the Vogini shop, Magli offers more of their conservative shoes at reasonable prices, but you'll still pay over $100 for really special pumps.

Two locations for Bruno in Venice. Behind San Marco.

**BRUNO MAGLI**, Frezzeria 1302 and 1583–85, San Marco

▼

**MISSONI:** Across from Bottega Veneta, this tiny shop is packed with Missoni's best. The shop is the size of a closet (a movie star's closet, not yours or mine—but you get the idea), but its size does not detract from the fact that it is crammed with merchandise. Sales are not nearly as good as in Milan.

**MISSONI**, Calle Vallaresso 1312B, San Marco

▼

**FRATELLI ROSSETTI:** Two shops in Venice to give you a tremendous selection of the Rossetti brothers' well-crafted shoes, boots, and handbags. The San Moisè shop may be the world's biggest Rossetti store. You can find pumps starting at $75 and boots at $150. The selection of men's shoes is grand. If you're going on to Milan and have the time for some off-the-beaten-track shopping, we do have the factory shop for you. Behind San Marco.

**FRATELLI ROSSETTI**
Salizzada San Moisè 1477
San Salvador 4800

▼

**TRUSSARDI:** If Trussardi's your "bag," this Venetian shop will offer you their usual complete selection of leathergoods, handbags, suitcases, and ready-to-wear in a multitude of styles. Not as much fun as the Paris shop, but the factory is nearby, so the City of Origin Axiom applies. Prices for ready-to-wear are shocking, but the colored leather accessories are very hot and very well priced.

**TRUSSARDI**, San Marco 695

## Shoes and Leathergoods

**BUSSOLA:** On the corner of San Luca, near the Rialto Bridge, this very modern boutique has lots of window space and displays and carries the most extensive collection of European designer leathergoods we've ever seen anywhere. Luggage freaks that we have become, we flipped our lids for the hard-sided Missoni luggage, with its leather-embossed roses in black on black. All major designer names, including Valentino, Ungaro, Krizia, and Les Must de Cartier.

**BUSSOLA**, San Marco 4608

▼

**LA FENICE:** If you love Maud Frizon, then this is the place for you! Although the prices are the same, we found the selection to be four times greater here than in Milan. The quality of merchandise also is better. A fabulous pair of evening shoes is $150; high-heeled pumps with open leather backs are $125. The man in your life also will walk away happily, with woven leather shoes priced at $120, and loafers for $125. Stéphane Kelian is next door.

**LA FENICE**, Via XXII Marzo 22

▼

**VOGINI:** Trust us! Have we got a shop (or two) for you. Vogini offers the best-looking designer-inspired handbags we've ever seen. They have woven styles, quilted styles, and everything that's hot or new. They ship, they take mail-order, they take plastic; they even defy the Italian mail service and get your packages to your door safely—we've always received our packages from them, usually within three weeks.

In the ladies' handbag section, there are shelves and shelves of bags. The quality of the leather is as good as Bottega if you get the baby calf bags. If you are trying to save money, get the calfskin bag, although you can feel the difference between the two. You will save considerably if you get calf instead of baby calf.

And speaking of money, there is no such thing as a cheap woven handbag. Drive that notion right out of your head. You can get a very small bag beginning at $100.

**VOGINI**, San Marco 1291–93

# Traditional Venetian Glass

**PAULY & COMPANY; SALVIATI & COMPANY:** The problem of where to get the best buys on the famous Venetian glass really is an empirical one. There are many shops but not very many fine artists.

The popular island of Murano (see page 119) has some of the famous workshops but for the most part is a tourist attraction, with second-rate merchandise. Maybe Aunt Kay won't know that the vase you bought was only $16, but maybe you overpaid! Everyone gets a commission for sending you to one place or another. Even your caring concierge probably has his "favorite" spot. One friend of ours took her concierge's advice to visit his favorite glass factory, and had a free gondola ride to the factory and a tour; but when she refused to buy anything because the quality was not to her expectations (she knew), the gondolier refused to take her back to her hotel! After much heated discussion, she was returned to the hotel, and the gondolier proceeded to yell at the concierge for wasting his time. Needless to say, everyone was embarrassed!

So if you're serious about glass, stick to these two factories. Pauly & Company has worked for most of the royal houses of Europe; Salviati & Company has won numerous design awards. Both are worth seeing, even if you are not buying. Pauly & Company will paint your glass to match your china. Both houses will ship and guarantee safe arrival of your purchases.

**PAULY & COMPANY**, Ponte dei Consorzi, San Marco

**SALVIATI & COMPANY**, San Gregorio 195

# Sporting Goods

**GRINTASPORT:** Conveniently located on the main shopping street, close to the Rialto Bridge. They carry the major Italian and French lines, Fila and Ellesse, as well as Nordica ski-wear. They are friendly and have an expert sales staff to assist you. Prices are excellent.

**GRINTASPORT**, Merceria San Salvador

▼

**ZETA SPORT:** Walk one street and one canal over from Merceria and follow the Calle dei Fabbri straight from Piazza San Marco to find Zeta Sport. The selection also is very good for Fila and Ellesse, and the prices are terrific. Zeta Sport has the best collection of kids' name-brand active sportswear in all Italy.

**ZETA SPORT**, Calle dei Fabbri 468

# Papergoods

Venice wouldn't be Venice without a ride in a gondola, a visit to the Doge's Palace, and a look-see at the handpainted paper. Leave your kids to chase the pigeons at San Marco while you go exploring.

You can find desk blotters, books, scrapbooks, and travel diaries, all covered in these unusual and beautiful papers. These items make the perfect gift for that person who has everything. If you're going on to Florence, there are more resources there; prices are slightly lower in Florence.

A few of our favorite papergoods shops in Venice are **EBRÛ,** San Marco 1920; **PAOLO OLBI,** San Marco 3653; and **LEGATORIA PIAZZESI,** Santa Maria del Giglio 2511.

*Legatoria* means bookbindery in Italian, and the famous designs are copies of bookbinding papers from hundreds of years ago. The best makers use the same old-fashioned methods that have been in the house for centuries. Many of the shops will make something to order for you, but ask up front if they will mail it for you; most won't. These papers have become so popular in the United States that the papergoods business now is divided between those who are staying old-fashioned and those who are counting the tourist bucks and loving it. When you walk into the various shops, you can feel the difference. There are many $10 gift items in these stores. A calendar-diary of the fanciest sort costs $50.

# Masks

I f you saw the movie or play *Amadeus,* you are familiar with the type of mask worn at Carnival time in Venice. Carnival in Venice got so out of hand that it was outlawed in 1797. But it's back again, and with it a renewed interest in masks. One of the most popular styles is the mask covered with bookbinding paper that you can find at a *legatoria,* or papergoods store (above). But there also are masks made of leather, papier-mâché, fabric, etc. After three days in Venice, you'll swear you'll die if you see another mask—so make your selection carefully. Many of them seem like trite tourist items. For a more special item, try any (or all!) of these famous maskmakers: **LE MASCHIERE DI DARIO USTINO,** Ponte dei Dai 171; **ADRIANO MIANI,** Calle Grimani 289B; **LABORATORIO ARTIGIANO MASCHIERE,** San Marco 282; **BRUNO RIZZATO,** Ponte dei Barcoli 1831; and **MA BOUTIQUE,** Calle Larga San Marco 282.

# Gifts

**LINDA MARIA GONZALES:** On the far side of the Rialto, this tiny shop is our single best resource for unique gifts. You have to like the look of marbleized paper; if you don't, skip on to another listing. This artist takes the same process and applies it to ceramics—mostly picture frames, but also all sorts of small objects. There're picture frames, boxes, and some small animals. They will pack for you—free.

**LINDA MARIA GONZALES,** Ruga Rialto 1035

▼

**VENEZIARTIGIANA:** If you must do all your shopping in a half hour, go to Veneziartigiana, which is rather a gallery for all the local artisans. Linda Maria Gonzales's work is sold here, as is the work of many, many other craftspeople. The shop, an artists' consortium, is "beside San Marco," one block before Merceria on the clock tower side.

**VENEZIARTIGIANA,** Calle Larga 412, San Marco

▼

**RAIGATTIERI:** Near San Stefano, this shop specializes in faience. It's a two-part shop: One part is country dishes, and one part is more traditional ceramics. A faience plate will cost about $25, and they will pack it for travel.

**RAIGATTIERI**, San Marco 3562

# Venice on a Schedule

When in Venice, do as the Venetians do: Walk. This is the only way to see Venice, no matter how limited your time may be. If you have unlimited funds and wish to see the art and also shop, we suggest you hire a guide. Venice is very small, but it is crammed with fine art and shops. The streets are not laid out in any logical order, and to see everything, expert guidance could save you a lot of aggravation. Ask your concierge for his suggestion, and ask the price before you hire anyone. You will also be expected to pick up lunch (sometimes costly), so count this into the price you figure. If you are on a limited budget but are splurging on the guide, tell him your budget for lunch *before* you enter a restaurant, or pick a pizza parlor or someplace you've already visited. We've heard way too many horror stories of people being "taken" to lunch—Watch out!

If you are more of a do-it-yourself person, we have a tour worked out for you. Remember that finding an address in Venice can be very tricky, since many of the buildings do not have numbers on them. If you feel frustrated, go into a shop and ask for your location by shop name, not by address. Venice is a small city, and usually everyone knows where everything else is.

## Tour 1: Piazza-to-Piazza All-Day Tour

This tour will take you through the main shopping areas of Venice. We are not including the glass factories in this day because going to the islands of Murano and Burano is a day tour in itself.

1. Begin your day at the Piazza San Marco. Walk completely around the *piazza,* under the covered portico. There aren't too many shops here, but the few that exist are special.

2. Find the Merceria, which is a street leading away from the *piazza* in a relatively straight line, toward the Rialto Bridge. Use this street as your guiding point only. Take side trips down streets that look interesting. Every time we take this trip, we find another new street. Continue to wind your way toward the Rialto Bridge. If done well, this area alone will take you more than half the day. Once you reach Riva del Carbon, take a right and you will be at the foot of the Rialto Bridge.

3. Cross the bridge, but don't shop yet! Enjoy all the fruits and vegetables at the market and the small shops tucked here and there. Visit Coin Rialto to see the architecture.

4. Walk back along Ruga Rialto and stop in any of the charming little boutiques that interest you. Make sure to check out Linda Maria Gonzales.

5. Cross back over the bridge and buy what looks good. At least now you know what you couldn't get for less on the other side.

6. Wind your way back to the Piazza San Marco along the Merceria. Believe it or not, you will notice things coming back that you didn't see going.

7. Spend your last savings not on a souvenir but on tea or a drink at Harry's Bar—it has to be experienced before you collapse.

## Tour 2: Island-Hopping All Day

You can do this as one big adventure, or as two little ones on different days. If you are in Venice in winter, separate the tours into two morning events, since the fog and mist come in so early in the afternoon.

1. The island of Burano is a famous fishing village. Fishermen make nets to catch their fish. Where there are netmakers, there are lacemakers. While the lace made in Burano is sold in Venice, it's much more fun to come to the island, where the prices are a bit cheaper, and you get a lot of local color. You can get to Burano by steamer from the Fondamenta Nuove. It takes about forty-five minutes each way. Few tourists take this adventure, so you'll probably have a great time. Just don't expect too many people to speak English.

2. You can also get to the island of Murano from the Fondamenta Nuove—this trip takes only about fifteen minutes. Murano is visited much more frequently than Burano, and has all the trappings of a tourist trap. The glass factories here put plenty of pressure on you to buy, and they can get rude if you take their time and then don't buy. We've never found the outstanding quality we were looking for, but enjoy the chase nonetheless. If your time is precious, skip this outing. There is also a glassworks museum in the middle of all this, if you have the kids with you or want to take in a little culture.

3. *Option:* We know that we're all about shopping, so forgive us this transgression, but if it's summer and we're traveling with our kids, we make a circle of a few islands and end up

at the beach at the Lido. All the usual beach things are for sale at the Lido, and you can rent a cabana or use the bathhouse for clothes changing. There're also some stores—use your CIGA card for discounts galore.

# 7 ▼ FLORENCE (FIRENZE)

## Welcome to Florence

T ravel agents will tell you that Florence is as popular as it is because of all the art treasures housed there—all the palaces and statues and masterpieces and fountains and churches and all that culture. They remind you of the magnificent light, and of the Arno River gracefully winding its way under medieval bridges. Rarely do they tell you that on top of all *that,* there is some truly great shopping.

It's not the classic *haute* shopping like that of Paris, or even London. It's not the hard-nosed business fashion that you find in Milan. Instead, Florence offers a charming, country-elegant shopping paradise that combines every element we love—boutiques representing the hottest designers in the world, trendy local shops offering the best of finely crafted gift items, several flea markets, and a fabulous old bridge jammed with teeny-tiny jewelry shops. The city reverberates with a total feeling of Old World delight that makes every minute you spend in Florence add value to the price of your purchase. It also reverberates with tourists, so don't be shocked if the crass gets mingled with the charm.

If you're in Florence for a short time, you will undoubtedly have to make lists of priorities so you can work in as much as possible—saving the rest for a return trip you will be committed to making. If one's time for shopping is truly limited to perhaps two or three hours' total, then we suggest you blow it all at the main flea market—the area from the Piazza Madonna around to San Lorenzo Church—where we've found some of our very best buys in leathergoods, gift items, designer scarves (probably fake), and costume jewelry. It's also a good place for jeans, casual clothes, and kids' fashions.

There is a good amount of fashion business in and around Florence. Many American department stores have buying offices there; the best department-store buyers and buying-office honchos always stop over in Florence to see what's available. Before Milan became the ready-to-wear capital it is now, the national fashion capital was indeed Florence. The Pitti Palace—once the home of the Medici—housed all the big fashion shows. (There still are several held there each year—Pitti Bimbo is the children's wear show; Pitti Uomo, the menswear show; and Pitti Casa, the housewares show.) There are factories outside of Florence, and fashion mavens who commute between Florence and Milan so they can have the best of both worlds.

# Booking Florence/1

**W**hile there are plenty of guides to the art treasures of Florence, and books (and even movies) about being in Florence, there aren't too many shopping guides. The Savoy Hotel does have a unique freebie, a small bound paperback called *Firenze Style*, which is a fancy version of a hotel giveaway, but it is devoted to retail advertising and to addresses of shops, with a small section on restaurants. It's written in English and Italian.

For guidebooks, or any books, be sure to visit the BM Bookshop (Borgo Ognissanti 4), which is stocked with books in English. It's a block from the Excelsior Hotel, and is run by an American woman who is married to a Florentine. The store not only carries English and American books, but has the course materials for over twenty different American university programs in Florence.

# Booking Florence/2

*P*ensiones are popular in Florence. If you want to stay in one, give a call to Jacques de Larsay, Inc. (800-366-1510), who represents many small hotels in Florence as well as some *pensiones* and is our unofficial but personal broker for cute little hotels. We always go back to old favorites, which we've rated for you as inexpensive (under $100 per night), moderate ($100–$150 per night), and expensive (over $150 per night):

**EXCELSIOR HOTEL/GRAND HOTEL:** These are two different CIGA hotels across the street from each other, each completing the other's half of the equation for a deluxe hotel. If you want the small version of the deluxe, you take the Grand. If you want the big, you go for the Excelsior. It's "in" to complain about how noisy the Excelsior is, or to ask for a room on a high floor, away from the River Arno; these are the most quiet rooms. We always ask for a river view—since that's what we came for. We personally think the Excelsior is one of the most beautiful hotels in the world. If you're going to be wild and crazy and splurge for a hotel like this just once in your life, this could be the one. Expensive. U.S. reservations, (800) 221-2340.

**GRAND HOTEL**, Piazza Ognissanti 1 (Telephone: 278781)

**EXCELSIOR HOTEL**, Piazza Ognissanti 3 (Telephone: 264201)

**SAVOY HOTEL:** We never really understood how all of Florence connected together until we stayed at the Savoy, which is the ultimate shopper's hotel. It's right in the middle of everything, and next door to the Duomo as well. An old-fashioned grand hotel, the Savoy is a member of the Leading Hotels of the World chain and has suites for kings and presidents. The best location in town. Expensive. U.S. reservations, (800) 223-6800.

**SAVOY HOTEL,** Piazza della Repubblica 7 (Telephone: 283313)

▼

**LUNGARNO:** If you want to be right in the middle of the shopping but on the Pitti Palace side of the Arno; if you want the most charming little hotel in Florence at a fabulous price; if you want to wake up with the river outside your room—the Lungarno is for you. Many of the rooms are duplexes; all are decorated in country elegance and simplicity. Ask specifically for a room with a river view. Moderate. U.S. reservations, (800) 223-1510.

**LUNGARNO,** Borgo San Jacopo 14 (Telephone: 264211)

## Getting There

**W**hile we always arrive by train, you can come by plane and take a bus or train directly from the Pisa airport to Florence. Or have a car and driver pick you up in Pisa and drive you to Florence.

# Getting Around

I t's a good thing you can walk just about everywhere in Florence, because more and more bans are being put on vehicular traffic. You can get a taxi at the train station, but this is a city for walkers. There is public transportation—should you be staying at the Jolly Hotel, which is a little farther away than some other hotels, you can take a bus to town. (You can also walk; it's not that far.) For your day trip to Siena (see page 174), you'll want to take the SITA bus. The SITA station is across the street from the train station, and an easy walk from most hotels.

If you want to drive a car into the surrounding countryside, you'll find prices are moderate. We always rent from Europcar, partly because their offices are next door to the Grand Hotel (Borgo Ognissanti 120r). Please note that rental rates are high unless you have bought into a promotional rate in the U.S.

While walking around town, notice that addresses have numbers in red or black. Red numbers are for retail establishments; black is for residences.

# Hours

L ike all of Italy, Florence closes at lunchtime. But it doesn't close tight. You can find some life if you look for it. Shops are also closed Sunday and Monday. Some stores open on Monday after lunch; ask your concierge to call first, if you have a specific shop in mind. Markets always close for holidays but do not necessarily close for lunch. If one of our listings remains open during lunch, we have so noted; otherwise, consider it closed.

## Sunday Shopping

S unday isn't a big shopping day in most of Italy, but if the weather is nice, or if the tourists are in season, you'd be surprised at just how much business is going on. While very few stores are open, the Straw Market does have sellers who open up their carts. But the real action is on the Ponte Vecchio. The usual shops are indeed shuttered, but on the walkway over the bridge, lining both sides of the walk, standing shoulder to shoulder, are an incredible array of vendors—from boys with imitation Louis Vuitton tote bags to hippies with poorly made jewelry to real artisans with crafts pieces. Much of what you will see here is delightful junk—the exact kind of thing you want to see on a Sunday. But there are a few buys.

*Tip:* Know your local prices before you jump at a "good deal." We passed up a wonderful deal on a Best Co. sweater because we thought $50 was high. Turns out this sweater costs $150 everywhere else. We bought a certain style canvas-and-leather tote for $100 (after much bargaining) and were delighted with ourselves. The next business day we saw this same tote in every leather store in town, for less than $100.

# Sending It Home

Although we have all been schooled to be nervous about the Italian mail system, we have had very good luck with a select group of Florentine retailers. We are no longer nervous to ask them to mail to us, and we have ventured to use the big post office, about two blocks from the Excelsior, where they have what's called Express Mail, which has worked for us. We still don't ship ourselves the crown jewels, but we do send home handbags, linens, and shoes.

# Scams and Rip-Offs

While Florence is not a high-crime city by any means, it is a very sophisticated city where many people come to shop and trade goods. As a result, the usual international deals and scams abound:

▼ Be wary of Etruscan art that's too good to be true—it is the most highly imitated art form sold in Italy.

▼ Don't be taken by the notion that if a store says it has a factory on the premises, it is a factory outlet and therefore is cheaper; many of those factories are just for show.

▼ If you are taken to a factory or a resource by your tour director, you may expect that a kickback is involved. Ask for free time to do your own exploring. On the other hand, maybe the tour director is taking you to a great place.

# Neighborhoods

As you know, if you've read one of our other books, we give different neighborhoods nicknames, so the names we have chosen for a neighborhood may not be technically correct—but they will get you there and will clearly delineate a trading area to you. This way you can get a grip on a part of the city mentally and know where you are and what there is to see and to buy.

## Tornabuoni *also via della vigna nuova*

The Via de' Tornabuoni is the main street for the mainline tourist shopping that we do so well; this is where most of the big-name designers have their shops, where the cute little specialty stores and leathergoods makers cluster. If you have only one hour for seeing the best shopping in Florence, perhaps you just want to stroll this street. (Then again, perhaps you just want to go to the San Lorenzo Market ... decisions, decisions!) Although most of the hotsy-totsy names are on Tornabuoni, some of them are in the area on side streets. So we call the whole neighborhood Tornabuoni, figuring that one good turn deserves another. The Tornabuoni area begins (or ends) at the Piazza Trinità, which is a small *piazza* with a very tall, skinny obelisk. The Via de' Tornabuoni itself sort of segues into Via della Vigna Nuova, which is another street with a lot of good shops and therefore is part of the Tornabuoni neighborhood (at least to us). Also see Via Strozzi, the connector between Tornabuoni and the Piazza della Repubblica.

# Florence

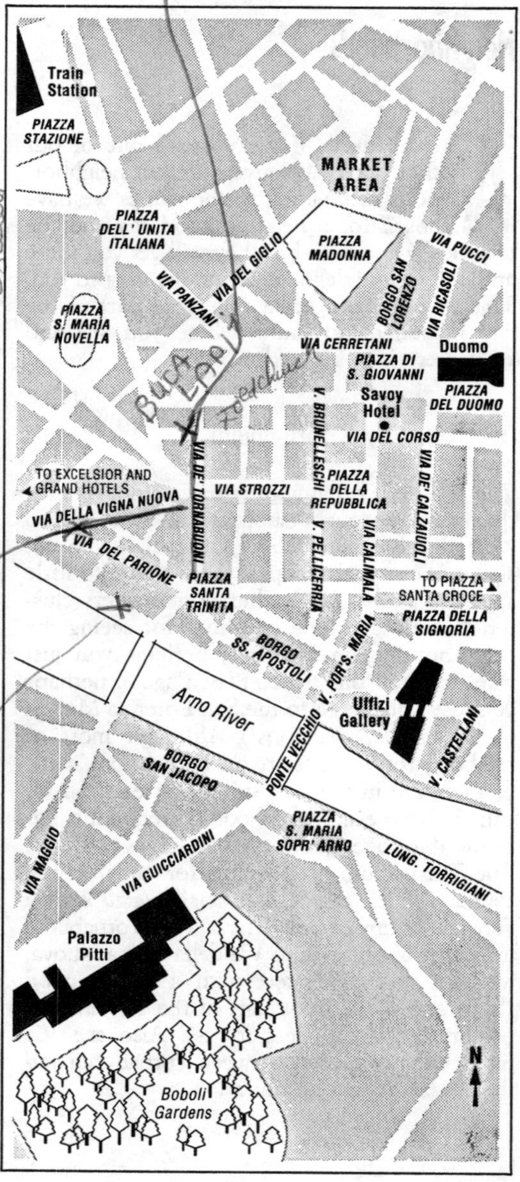

Handwritten annotations on map:

great restaurant is down — OMERO

ver Santa Elisabetta

dritta large

American Graffiti — womans clothes — great price 2 floors

John F. Sophia

BUCA LAPPI

Train Station
PIAZZA STAZIONE

MARKET AREA

PIAZZA DELL' UNITA ITALIANA

PIAZZA MADONNA

VIA PUCCI

VIA PANZANI

VIA DEL GIGLIO

PIAZZA S. MARIA NOVELLA

BORGO SAN LORENZO

VIA RICASOLI

VIA CERRETANI

PIAZZA DI S. GIOVANNI

Duomo

Savoy Hotel

PIAZZA DEL DUOMO

V. BRUNELLESCHI

VIA DEL CORSO

VIA DE' CALZAIUOLI

TO EXCELSIOR AND GRAND HOTELS

VIA DE' TORNABUONI

VIA STROZZI

PIAZZA DELLA REPUBBLICA

VIA DELLA VIGNA NUOVA

V. PELLICCERIA

VIA CALIMALA

VIA DEL PARIONE

PIAZZA SANTA TRINITA

TO PIAZZA SANTA CROCE

PIAZZA DELLA SIGNORIA

BORGO SS. APOSTOLI

V. POR S. MARIA

Arno River

Uffizi Gallery

V. CASTELLANI

BORGO SAN JACOPO

PONTE VECCHIO

PIAZZA S. MARIA SOPR' ARNO

LUNG. TORRIGIANI

VIA MAGGIO

VIA GUICCIARDINI

Palazzo Pitti

Boboli Gardens

N

144

## Excelsior Grand

This is by no means the real name of this neighborhood. The real name is Piazza Ognissanti. Each side of this *piazza* is flanked by a large and very grand hotel—the Excelsior on one side and the Grand on the other. Easy as pizza pie. The Excelsior Grand neighborhood backs up to Tornabuoni, so there are lots of stores here. Many good stores are actually on Piazza Ognissanti; the rest line Via Ognissanti until it hits Piazza Goldini and segues into Via della Vigna Nuova. If all this sounds confusing, don't panic. The two neighborhoods are close to each other and could even be considered one neighborhood, except that to us they have two different characters. The shops in the Excelsior Grand area are less touristy and more mom-and-pop than the big names over in Tornabuoni, and the prices may be a few cents cheaper off the bigger streets. That's all. This still is primary shopping, and it is grand.

## Excelsior Grand Antiques

There are two main antiques areas in Florence, one near the Pitti Palace and the other right beside the Excelsior Grand area at Piazza Ognissanti. If your back is to the Excelsior, on your left is the Arno River and on your right is a church. Pass a small street called Via del Porcellana, then look across Borgo Ognissanti, to the shop **FIORETTO GIAMPAOLO** (No. 43r). Visit it, then walk a block toward Tornabuoni until you get to the Piazza Goldini. Here is the Via dei Fossi, which is crammed with antiques dealers. In fact, the area between the two streets and including the Via del Moro, which runs next to Via dei Fossi, is host to almost two dozen dealers. Most of these stores sell larger pieces of furniture and medium-to-important antiques; there is not too much junk. There are some businesses that are geared to the design trade, without being in the antiques business—such as **RICCARDO BARTHEL**, who does tiles (Via de Fossi 11r). In the fall (ask your concierge for the exact day, since it varies from year to year) there is one Sunday that is open house for all dealers in the area. Among the big-time, fancy dealers here, try: **GALLERIA LUIGI BELLINI,** Lungarno Soderini 5; **BARTO-LOZZI & FIGLIO,** Rosso Via Maggio 18; **GALLORI TURCHI,** Via Maggio 14r; **PAOLO ROMANO,** Borgo Ognissanti 20r; and **PAOLA FALLANI,** Borgo Ognissanti 15r.

## The Duomo

There is a Duomo in Florence as well as in Milan. This, too, is a magnificent church. Its architectural style is totally different from the Duomo in Milan (Milan is Gothic; Florence is Romanesque), and once you've seen the two churches you will not get either the buildings or the shopping areas confused. As in Milan, there is excellent shopping around the Duomo. Naturally, this is an older, more traditional area. Most of these stores are in older buildings. Locals as well as tourists shop here. The main shopping street is called Via de' Calzaiuoli. It is closed to street traffic so pedestrians can wander freely from the Duomo to Piazza della Signoria, another large *piazza* filled with pigeons, incredible fountains and statues, and tourists and locals and charm and glamour and everything you think Florence should have. You can't rave about an area too much more than that, can you? The shopping street that connects the Duomo to the Ponte Vecchio (Via Roma) runs past Piazza della Repubblica, where many traditional stores are located. The Savoy Hotel is on this corner. Via Roma becomes Via Por Santa Maria. Don't miss **LUISA VIA ROMA,** at Via Roma 21.

## Ponte Vecchio

If you keep walking a few hundred meters from Piazza della Signoria right to the banks of the River Arno, you will see the Ponte Vecchio. You'll zig to the right a few yards and then walk across the bridge. The area we call Ponte Vecchio includes just the bridge and the retailers on the Duomo side of the bridge. Once you cross over the bridge and get to the other side, you are in another neighborhood. Ponte Vecchio is a distinct neighborhood, however, because the entire bridge is populated by jewelry shops. They are tiny little shops that have been there for centuries in one form or other. The ones on the Duomo side of the bridge are fancier than the ones closer to the other side, and prices are cheaper as you move over the bridge. If you are standing on the Duomo side, about to cross over the bridge, the shops on the right-hand side also are nicer than the shops on the left-hand side. They sell a little of everything, but you can find nice gift items and trinkets here. You needn't be looking for a diamond to match Elizabeth Taylor's. On Sundays, when shopping opportunities in Florence are limited, the bridge is crammed with vendors who sell everything from handcrafted jewelry to leather goods that imitate name brands.

## Over the Bridge

Once you cross over the Ponte Vecchio, you reach a different retailing climate. You are now on the Pitti side of the bridge. The stores are smaller and less touristy; you get the feeling that "real people" also shop here. You can wander, discovering your own personal finds; you can stop and get the makings of a picnic. The shopping goes in two directions: toward the Pitti or along the Arno. See both areas, looking at shops on Borgo San Jacopo and on Via Guicciardini.

# The Big Names

**ALEX:** Alex is one of the best stores in Florence for designer clothes. Well-stocked with a good selection of Alaïa, Thierry Mugler, Claude Montana, Gianni Versace, Byblos, Complice, Genny, and Basile.

**ALEX**, Via della Vigna Nuova 5 and 19

▼

**GIORGIO ARMANI:** Armani has stocked this shop with a large and terrific selection. The store is on two levels: The front part is for men, the back is for women. Sales in the store are discreet but worthwhile. The price tags are very simply marked over without any announcement of a storewide clearance. What class.

The newer Emporio shop incorporates the famous Doney Café, in a new location, with a new lease on life, via Armani.

**GIORGIO ARMANI**, Via de' Tornabuoni 35–37
**ARMANI EMPORIO**, Piazza Strozzi

▼

**BELTRAMI:** Beltrami is one of Florence's best-known wonder stories—the leather and shoe people who made it big. They have several stores in town, and are expanding on their tradition of opening up a villalike store in each community. The newest shop in Florence is on Tornabuoni, and is indeed an old villa redone in modern style but still dripping with Old World elegance.

The older Beltrami stores have charm and

heavy crystal chandeliers; the outlet store has no charm whatsoever, but is an interesting source for last year's shoes and boots. The outlet looks like a real dive—you would surely walk by if you didn't know what it was—but the shoes are arranged by men's and women's and by color groups, so if you find your size, you might find a deal for $60. Since the location is right in town, you lose nothing in stopping by to see if you can get lucky.

**BELTRAMI**
    Via de' Tornabuoni 48r
    Via de' Calzaiuoli 31r
    Via de' Calzaiuoli 44r
**BELTRAMI OUTLET**, Via Panzani 1

▼

**LAURA BIAGIOTTI:** Biagiotti is pricey: Dresses start at $400 but are a savings on the U.S. prices. Biagiotti is known for her cashmere knits. We think the best part of the Florence shop is the stained-glass inset in the front doors—watercolor pastels in a graphic design.

**LAURA BIAGIOTTI**, Via Calimala 27r

▼

**BOTTEGA VENETA:** This shop is gorgeous and well-stocked. We found all the Bottega luggage here—we have not seen Bottega luggage in any of the other shops around Italy. The store has a mezzanine in the back that often offers promotional sales. Perhaps the best Bottega store in Italy. Next door to the Grand Hotel.

**BOTTEGA VENETA**, Piazza Ognissanti 3

▼

**CÉLINE:** The Céline boutique in Florence is very small, especially if you've ever seen their Roman digs. Yet this is the shop that told us a very interesting tidbit. Their secret: Much of the line is made in Italy. These items are cheaper in the Florence shop than in Paris. Ask, and the world is yours. Also visit Athos for more Céline bargains (see page 157).

**CÉLINE**, Via de' Tornabuoni 61–63

▼

**COLE-HAAN:** Yep, this is the American shoe firm you already know and love, and nope, this is not a standard case of an American company opening shop in Europe. Cole-Haan makes a lot of their shoes in Italy, so what you've got is more of a local outlet. This is the only store with the complete collection including the U.S.- and Italian-made shoes—so don't buy the U.S.-made ones here. But do grab the $100 mocs in buttery soft Italian leather.

If you have hard-to-fit feet, fret no more—the store does custom work and serves many basketball players. They'll charge you about $30 to airmail your shoes to you one month after you order them—not bad at all! Those who love Ralph Lauren–style low-cut loafers and mocs should make a special trip to Florence just for this store.

**COLE-HAAN**, Via de' Tornabuoni 77r

▼

**ENRICO COVERI:** We're nuts for the Coveri shops—the architecture is always amusing. Here there are five interconnecting rooms housing the entire collection. The interiors are all New Italian, with ash wood, and orange metallic finishes, and tables that have upside-down triangular legs in orange laminates. Don't miss the room of children's things.

**ENRICO COVERI**, Via della Vigna Nuova 27–29
**ENRICO COVERI COUTURE**, Via de' Tornabuoni 81r

▼

**FENDI:** What a zoo! In summer, every American within shouting distance of Florence stands in line to get the next Fendi bargain. Then you have your basic Italians who are hot on emotion and like to wave their arms, wag their fingers, and shout at the manager. The selection is small, and we suggest you wait for Rome, where even though you will also fight crowds, you will see something very special as well.

**FENDI**, Via de' Tornabuoni 27r

▼

**SALVATORE FERRAGAMO:** Yes, there are Ferragamo shops all over Italy and all over the world. But none of them comes near the parent shop in Florence, which is in a building erected in 1215, complete with vaulted ceilings, stained-glass windows, and enough ambience to bring out your camera. The shop has several connecting antechambers with an incredible selection of shoes, boots, and ready-to-wear. Shoe sizes are American.

Believe it or not, old Signor Salvatore Ferragamo started in Hollywood and then went back to Italy after the Crash. Ferragamo's widow runs the business while daughter Fiamma designs the women's line; brothers and sisters also are in shoe biz, in the offices upstairs in the *palazzo*.

Downstairs, in the shop, you are fitted, with a real honest-to-goodness tortoiseshell shoehorn. Prices are about 30% less than in the

United States. There are no steals here—expect to pay $100 to $150 for a pair of shoes—but the workmanship and detailing are excellent. High-fashion shoes are much more.

In January and July there's a clear-it-all-out sale that is worth a special trip overseas.

**SALVATORE FERRAGAMO**, Via de' Tornabuoni 16

▼

**FRETTE:** The linen store is now located in Pratesi's old store.

**FRETTE**, Lungarno Vespucci 8–10

▼

**FURLA:** A small shop, but stocked with Furla handbags and accessories. The styles are always ahead of their time and designed with a sense of humor. Prices are moderate to high. There are some two dozen stores all over Italy (and two in New York), but this is one of the most convenient to high-traffic shopping areas. The street is a connector between the two main shopping streets of the Duomo area.

**FURLA**, Via de' Tosinghi 5r

▼

**GUCCI:** There are two Gucci shops, a few doors apart, in Florence. One is the original Gucci, where all those little G's were born; the other is a brand-new splash of money and marble and golden crocodile jewelry. There is an incredible selection of merchandise here, but it's not easy to make your choices; the older store has many different little rooms, with handbags in each. While the bags are separated by color or texture, you can't see all of them at one time, so you can't compare your purchase to see if you've found all the choices.

Now then, the bigger problem. To buy at Gucci, or not to buy at Gucci? Gucci and Gucci-like merchandise are sold all over town. If you go into the Gucci shop to try to see if you can find the same items, you may discover that you cannot. Then, a week later, you find the exact thing in out-of-town official Gucci outlets. The merchandise in the flagship Florence store is changed more frequently than anywhere else, specifically because of the problem with unauthorized imitations. Gucci does not like all those fakes out there. But they cannot stop them. You are on your own as to where you buy your G's—there are savings everywhere.

One of the best things about Gucci in Florence is the range of incredibly inventive merchandise you may not see in other locations—Gucci everything, from ice tongs to fire tongs. Good gifts for the person who has everything.

**GUCCI**, Via de' Tornabuoni 73

▼

**MAX MARA:** We've watched Max grow from a small name to a big one, with a complete Max Mara line and the SportMax line, as well as a few other homegrown lines sold in the shop. This is the best of designer sportswear, rather the Calvin Klein of Italy. There are stores in all the Italian cities, so your selection will be good just about everywhere. But we like to make our biggest haul in Florence, so we send you here where the sales are great and the styles are classic enough to last many years. Around the corner from the Duomo, on the way to the train station.

**MAX MARA**, Via Brunelleschi 28r

▼

**PINEIDER:** Do you love to send handwritten notes in the mail? The kind sent on thick formal cards that smell of old money and inseparable style? Pineider supplies Cartier with many of its papers. Be sure to shop for your Christmas cards early. You'll find very conservative, old-time cards in just a few styles. Prices are steep. Prints are sold upstairs.

**PINEIDER**
  Piazza della Signoria 13
  Via de' Tornabuoni 76r

▼

**EMILIO PUCCI:** Emilio Pucci is alive and well and still doing the same thing—all those little geometrics. And they're still the rage. His couture line is well respected, and his headquarters are in Florence in a very, very imposing building on the far side of the Duomo. The firm has been bought by an American company, but Mr. Pucci is still designing and has brought his daughter, Laudimia, into the business. She handles the couture. Very hot Retro look.

**EMILIO PUCCI**, Palazzo Pucci, Via dei Pucci 6

▼

**RASPINI:** Even if you haven't heard of it, there may not be a bigger name in Florence retailing circles. Raspini owns the Armani shop (the door says *Raspini per Armani*) as well as several funky little shops and one or two really big and important establishments. The flagship store is on the Via Roma and sells many designer lines, from Chanel to Prada, for men and women. It's a very modern, elegant shop with high prices and fancy clients. While Raspini is best known first for shoes, and then for leathergoods, this store proves the crossover connection into big-name retailing.

**RASPINI**
Via Roma 25r
Via Por Santa Maria 72 (shoes only)

▼

**MARINA RINALDI:** A designer look that is traditional but more modern than preppy. This is a designer line in large sizes; you can add on a piece at a time and end up with a full closet of coordinating clothes—from jeans to coats. There is also a dress-up line. Sizes go up to an American 24, which is 56 in Italy.

**MARINA RINALDI,** Via de' Calzaiuoli 14r

▼

**TRUSSARDI:** Rapid expansion is the name of the game, and Nicolo Trussardi is amazing the world with all the new shops he has opened up and with the amount of merchandise that is filling them. We think Trussardi still is best as a resource for luggage, small leathergoods, handbags, and their special impregnated canvas with leather trim—but you also can get ready-to-wear for men, women, and kids. This shop is most special because of the vaulted, frescoed ceiling with the neomodern wipe lights and the piped-in classical music.

**TRUSSARDI,** Via de' Tornabuoni 34–36

▼

**VALENTINO:** The Valentino shop in Florence is nice, as are all Valentino boutiques, and has a large selection of couture and GFT-made Valentino. Many European Valentino boutiques do not sell the cheaper (GFT) lines that Mr. V makes—Miss V, Night, etc.—and we love these lines, since we can afford them when they are on sale. This store carries all Valentino brands and accessories. Prices are 20% to 30% off U.S. prices; sales are even better. If you're offended by our talk of less expensive lines, here you go: You can buy a sweater set and skirt—cashmere and wool, of course—for just under $2,000 from the regular Valentino line.

**VALENTINO**, Via della Vigna Nuova 47

▼

**GIANNI VERSACE:** What an exciting shop! What a thrill to see that old retailing hoopla come to Florence! Celebrate life just by looking at this two-story shop, with its sandblasted vaulted brick ceiling, ridged cement floors, and New Italian–style interior. This shop is magnificent. The clothing is expensive but considered well-priced for such top-of-the-line ready-to-wear. Expect to pay a couple of hundred dollars for a blouse.

**GIANNI VERSACE**, Via de' Tornabuoni 13–15

# China and Crystal

Florence is the last place in the world you'd go to buy your English china, but we have found good prices.

**ARMANDO POGGI:** This shop is very fancy—it's the kind of place you'd find a *contessa* shopping with her daughter for wedding china. Yet the prices are as good as Reject China's in London!

**ARMANDO POGGI**, Via de' Calzaiuoli 105 and 116

**RICHARD GINORI:** The factory is in Sesto, a small village about twenty minutes outside of Florence. Give it a try if you have a car, or don't mind taking a chance—cabs are cheap in Italy. Make sure the driver waits for you. There is an outlet shop.

**RICHARD GINORI,** Sesto

## Jewelry, Shoes, and Leathergoods

**BIJOUX CASCIO:** This is a small Florentine company that makes a lot of glitz and some serious imitations, and we think it's one of the very best finds in all of Europe. "Gold" chokers with "diamond" *pavé*, about $50; 36-inch-long chains—with jewels inlaid, natch—$60. The golden croc bracelet—copied from Gucci's window—$40. Each piece of jewelry is sold with its own fabric pouch to make sure it doesn't get scratched. Go nuts. Go wild. You'll never get another opportunity.

**BIJOUX CASCIO**
Via Por Santa Maria 1
Via de' Tornabuoni 32r

▼

**ATHOS:** If you are looking for an Hermès-style handbag, have we got a store for you. Prices are not inexpensive, but quality is high, and much of the work appears to be made for big-name retailers. This is a small, family-run business. They have a big scrapbook filled with thank-you notes from royalty and Hollywood stars. If this isn't enough to convince you that you've hit the find of the century, ask to see the tools—we saw the stamps that imprint the logos of every major French and Italian designer in the world. Athos is a jobber for these designers. Look for Valentino, Céline, and Hermès goods among the classics. Athos also does private-label work for many of the better U.S. department stores. Now that the Chanel bag is *de rigueur*, you'll find many styles here, although the catch is totally different from Chanel's. Donna Karan–style belts are also big.

**ATHOS**, Borgo SS. Apostoli 6

▼

**PARRI'S:** Across the bridge; don't miss upstairs and downstairs. Parri's is another of those shops that claim to have a factory on the premises—in this case it's next door, at No. 12. While prices are high, we've found that if you buy a lot, you can negotiate a better deal. We've also called Parri's from the United States and ordered items—the kind of things we were too dumb to buy the first time we saw them— and gotten good service and delivery. If the first floor doesn't interest you, go upstairs. It does get better. They will make gloves to measure in twenty-four hours.

**PARRI'S**, Via Guicciardini 18

▼

**MANTELASSI:** If made-to-measure is what you have in mind, step this way with your instep. Men and women can work on the design, bring a shoe to be copied, or choose from the many shoes already there.

**MANTELASSI**, Piazza della Repubblica 25r

▼

**TANINO CRISCI:** This is a chain of moderately priced shoes in sort of sporty, conservative styles. There's something a bit chunky about a lot of the styles that we don't like, but there are many worthwhile things here, especially for men. The quality is well known; the prices range from $140 to over $200. These are not no-name cheapie shoes. They are classics, and the older they get, the better they look.

**TANINO CRISCI**, Via de' Tornabuoni 43–45

▼

**FRANCO RIZZO:** For young, inexpensive shoes in the $50 range. Good location in the Duomo area.

**FRANCO RIZZO**, Via de' Calzaiuoli 3r

▼

**MELUSINE:** Despite the fact that the name of this store sounds like something kitchen counters should be made with, Melusine is an up-and-coming shoe and leathergoods luxury line, with a store in Florence and a store in Paris, that we expect will have more stores in more big cities as time goes by, because the designs are sensational. Classic and expensive, with just enough sense of fashion to let the world know you've got the right stuff. Note the hardware, elegant, simple, but expensive-looking. Pricey but distinctive.

**MELUSINE**, Via della Vigna Nuova 16r

▼

**BAJOLA:** If only Old World style will do it for you but you find Louis Vuitton too obvious, you probably want luggage from Bajola, which was founded in 1896. This is a very local kind of resource, the place the "in" society knows about that does not have a big American tourist business. Goody. It's across the street from the Beltrami outlet store.

**BAJOLA**, Via Rondinelli 25r

**CASADEI:** This is a wild shop with wild shoes. The interior is rather Greco-Roman, with taupe stone floors leading to a stone-and-tile try-on area, which is elevated by one step. In front of the back wall there are two bronze mermaids holding urns on their heads. The designs are very special; prices range from $150 to $250.

**CASADEI,** Via de' Tornabuoni 33r

*good prices* ▾

**MADOVA:** Gloves are back in style, so stock up at this maker of sublime gloves. We think the cashmere-lined, yellow, butter-soft leather ones make an excellent gift—$40. Unlined gloves are about $20 and come in about a million colors. There's everything here, from the kind of white kid gloves we used to wear in the 1960s to men's driving gloves to very ornately designed, superbly made high-button gloves. Over the Bridge.

**MADOVA,** Via Guicciardini 1

▾

**DESMO:** Desmo has made a name for itself as a maker of leather clothing and shoes and accessories, but what will most impress you in this shop is their need to copy someone else's work. If you are looking for a copy of the real thing, Desmo has that copy. They even copy shoe styles. Most of their work is stunning, the workmanship superb. The two-floor boutique is packed with handbags. There are noncopies as well, which are well-priced and well-made.

**DESMO,** Via de' Tornabuoni 18

FRANK F
JOHN F
LUNGARNO

leather coats, pants
good prices — negotia

# Papergoods

**BOTTEGA ARTIGIANA DEL LIBRO:** This is a small shop, next to the Arno, that has beautiful things and can solve many a gift quandary. This is the place we buy all those miscellaneous gift items for schoolteachers, etc. Small address books are in the $8 range; pencils are stunning and inexpensive; picture frames range from $5 to $15, depending on the size. These frames have plastic fronts, not glass. There are photo albums, bound blank books, and all sorts of other items. We love it here.

**BOTTEGA ARTIGIANA DEL LIBRO,** Lungarno Corsini 38–40

▼

**GIANNINI E FIGLIO:** Historically well-known for the marbleized type of paper, they've been in business for centuries. They also make bookplates, calling cards, and items for all other paper needs. Great gift item—several paper-wrapped pencils tied with a bow; the price obviously depends on how many pencils you buy, but you can put together a beautiful $10 package. If you go to the Pitti Palace (and it wouldn't be Florence without a trip to the Pitti Palace), you'll be right there—it's sort of an unofficial museum gift shop.

**GIANNINI E FIGLIO,** Piazza Pitti 37

▼

**IL PAPIRO:** The most commercially successful of the marbleized-paper stores, with branches all over Italy and even in the United States.

**IL PAPIRO,** Lungarno Acciaioli 112r

## Active Sportswear

Florence must have an awful lot of athletes, because there are tons of sporting goods shops there that sell equipment and active sportswear.

**CASA DELLO SPORT:** Our favorite because it has a huge selection at great prices and is right in a shopping area we never miss. We also have never forgotten the Snoopy ski parka we once, years ago, saw in the window. This is not a discount shop, but the prices were good enough for us not to care.

CASA DELLO SPORT, Via de' Tosinghi 8–10

There are also several shops, besides Casa dello Sport, with a great Fila selection. The Fila people have provided us with their list of sporting goods stores in Florence that carry a good selection of their merchandise. (Please check an address with your concierge, because it may not be in a tourist neighborhood.) We love Casa dello Sport because it is in a main shopping drag that we would go to regardless, but if you need a size or a style you are having trouble finding, this list may help you:

**LO SPORT,** Piazza Duomo 7
**IL RIFUGIO SPORT,** Piazza Ottaviani 3
**FRANCO SPORT,** Via Nazionale 109
**LO SPORT SHOPPING,** Via Masaccio 201
**CAMPING SPORT,** Via dei Servi 70–72

# Antiques in Florence

F lorence is the acknowledged center for antiquers in Italy. We've seen a few antiques at Montecatini, but that doesn't count. One of the best things about the home furnishings market in Florence is that everyone there—whether fabric supplier or antiques dealer—wants to sell you something. They are willing to make shipping arrangements, they will rarely give you a song and dance about their American distributor (well, maybe Knoll will), they will give you a trade discount if you present a business card and make a substantial order. They are in the business of doing business, and that's our kind of place.

As an antiques center, Florence gets a lot of pieces from the entire Tuscan area. The problems with fakes, which are so severe in Rome, are not so great here. Anyone can get taken, that's well known, but the chances are less in Florence than in Rome.

Antiques are available at a flea market at the Piazza dei Ciompi, but it's pretty junky. For serious stuff, check out: Via Guicciardini, Via Maggio, Via de' Tornabuoni, Via della Vigna Nuova, Via del Porcellana, Borgo SS. Apostoli, Via dei Fossi, Via del Moro, Via Santo Spirito, or Via della Spada.

# Gifts

**C. MOSCARDI:** A factory that makes a lot of the picture frames you see around town, Moscardi also will sell directly from their shop.

You can get anything, from the teeny-tiny Florentine gilt up to something grand and large. Shipping gets to be a problem if you get into really oversized, but we like the gift frames in silver or silverplate. Over the Bridge.

C. MOSCARDI, Lungarno Corsini 36

▼

**COSE DEL PASSATO:** As the name says, nice things from the past. We're freaks for faience, so we could spend the day here. There are other, easier-to-carry gifts as well.

COSE DEL PASSATO, Via dei Fossi 3–5

▼

**TRAVERSARI:** Another famous silver outlet. This one has formal silver jewelry in modern designs. The prices are excellent—a good pair of earrings for $35, a cuff bracelet for $85. Classic silver frames from $60 to $120. Although the store looks forbiddingly expensive when you walk by, the prices are very good. Don't be frightened off. Over the Bridge.

TRAVERSARI, Via Guicciardini 120

▼

**ANGELA CAPUTI:** Dynamite, creative fun in the costume jewelry category, with bright, colored plastics and lots of inventive twists and turns. We were tempted to buy out the shop or open a branch of our own. Prices range from $10 to $100. Caputi is well-known in designer circles as a hot talent, and now has young, modern clothes to go with her jewelry.

ANGELA CAPUTI, Borgo San Jacopo 82

*MERCATO CENTRALE*
*Food market—red roof*
*look up from the stalls*

# Markets

**SAN LORENZO:** Little thrills us the way a few hours in the San Lorenzo Market do. Of course, we love markets and the very nature of them—colors, smells, people, merchandise everywhere, pushcarts, bargains. You name it and San Lorenzo has it. Most specifically, San Lorenzo is good for fakes of big-name merchandise, cheap clothing for kids or teens, and cheap glitzy costume jewelry.

The market has a few pushcart dealers and then several rows of stalls that lead around a bend. The stalls are very well organized—this is a legal fair, and stallholders pay tax to the city. Many of the stalls give you shopping bags with their numbers printed on them. Now, there's class. With the recent crackdown on phony big-name merchandise, few of the pushcarts have their imitations out for display. If you are having a language problem, keep saying "Gucci?" If you have a Gucci item, take it out of your purse to make your point. We promise you that some of these guys have either hot or *faux* Gucci in their cars. It is not dirt cheap, by the way. Gucci wallets may cost $6 in Bangkok, but they cost $35 in the Florence market. (They cost more at Gucci.)

*A word of caution:* Do not get so excited with the bargains that you don't cast your eagle eye over the goods. Look for defects; look for details. We bought some Hermès scarves that later, back at the hotel, did not look like Hermès scarves at all—they were very poor copies. Stay calm. Many stallowners take plastic.

**STRAW MARKET:** The best thing about the Straw Market is that it doesn't close during lunchtime. It's also within walking distance of the Ponte Vecchio and the Duomo and all the other parts of Florence you want to see, so you can make your day itinerary and get it all in. Locals call this market *Porcellino,* in honor of the boar statue that stands here.

This market sells far more junk, far less of value to a local, and much more in the way of souvenirs than the other markets. At the Straw Market we always visit with Giuseppe Pugi Delli at Stand 2; he always has what we want. If he doesn't have what you want, he will get it. Got it? Good. The Straw Market is closed on Sunday and on Monday morning. During the season, some vendors open up on Sundays, but just five or six of them. It's still fun.

**SANT' AMBROGIO:** This is a local market that sells fruit and veggies and cheap clothes and sneakers and radios and is very nice if you're living there, but if you want Gianfranco Ferré on sale, we assure you this is not your kind of place. Piazza Ghiberi, weekday mornings.

**PIAZZA DEI CIOMPI:** It's the local flea market that sells everything from furniture to pictures to coins to jewelry, but it's a bit junky, and you might not find anything.

# Florence on a Schedule

F lorence is one of those cities you never have enough time in. Since we love markets and bargains as much as we love art and fountains, we're always in a quandary about where to go first and what to see next. If Botticelli's *Rites of Spring* is the most important part of your trip, go directly to the Uffizi Gallery; if your personal rite of spring is a new frock, try one of our tours.

## Tour I: Half-Day Delight

If you have only half a day for shopping, try part of our full-day extravaganza tour (Tour 2) so you can see all the big names, or relax and just wander around the San Lorenzo Market. You'll find everything you came to Italy for, at the best prices.

## Tour 2: Full-Day Florentine Extravaganza

1. Begin the tour at Ferragamo, at the Piazza San Trinità, at 9:30 A.M. Walk down Via de' Tornabuoni to see the designer boutiques.

2. Then walk across to Palazzo Antinori. When the street ends, cross it and take a right. At a teeny-tiny street to the left, turn left. Walk one block to Piazza Madonna. Go right at the Madonna and follow the stalls around both ways.

3. Explore the market area until exhausted or ready for lunch. You may want to return to your hotel to dump your packages. Most shops in Florence will close from 1 to 3:30 P.M., so if you want, this is your chance for lunch and a foot soak. *Or* stroll toward the Straw Market on the Por Santa Maria. The Straw Market is open during lunchtime. Walk back to Ponte Vecchio so you are on the bridge when the shops open after lunch at, say, 3:30 P.M.

4. Walk across the bridge on the right side of the street, visiting any of the tiny jewelry shops that meet your fancy. *Tip:* The stores are more expensive on the near side of the bridge, but less expensive as you get to the far side. Many of them sell the same merchandise. When you get to the other side of the Arno, walk down and back up Via San Jacopo; don't miss Angela Caputi. Then

walk back across the Arno on the right side of the bridge, which will be the side opposite the one you crossed on.

5. Once over the Arno, turn right on Lungarno Generale Díaz. Please note that the main drag running along the Arno changes its name at every bridge, so while you've probably been on the street before—and will be again later in the day—its name will change and you may get confused. Walk to the Uffizi, stopping in any of the shops if they interest you. Take in the beautiful view of the river.

6. Once at the Uffizi, turn left into the courtyard and walk across to the Piazza della Signoria, which has a fabulous fountain, some cute little horse and buggies, and a zillion tourists. Cross the *piazza* to Via de' Calzaiuoli, a famous shopping street. No cars are allowed here.

7. The street is about three blocks long and ends at the Duomo. Circle behind the Duomo and walk or taxi to Ponte Vecchio.

8. Once at Ponte Vecchio, stay on the main river drag and follow it until you get to the Excelsior Hotel. You'll pass many of our favorite boutiques and several paper shops.

9. Take a break at the Excelsior for tea—or strong coffee. This is one of our favorite hotels in Florence, and whether you stay here or not, drop in to check out the digs. If you prefer your tea break to be a little more native, there's a little supermarket across Piazza Ognissanti from the hotel where you can get some fresh bread and cheese and have a picnic while looking out at the river. You may now choose to bail out of the extravaganza tour, or continue.

10. Of course you're going on! Choice A is to return to the flea market at San Lorenzo and buy whatever you didn't buy there in

the morning, now that you know the lay of the land and have seen a tremendous amount of retail goods. If you go back, treat yourself to a taxi from the front of the Excelsior. If you have no reason to return to San Lorenzo, turn right at the front of the hotel and begin to explore all the little boutique-filled streets that form the web from the main bridge streets. The stores will be open until 7:30 P.M., the flea market until 8 P.M. You will have earned your pasta for dinner after this tour!

## Tour 3: The Antiques Stroll

1. Begin by crossing Ponte Vecchio to the far side of the bridge. The bridge is an antique in itself.

2. Stroll down Via Guicciardini—the main street as you come off the bridge—and head toward the Pitti Palace. As you walk you will be tempted to shop for silver or leathergoods, but try to control yourself—this is the antiques tour, remember?

3. First stop is Giacomo Chiarantini (No. 7), which sells old books, prints, furniture, and old vases—but the prints are the specialty of the house. Continue looking at whatever interests you on the street.

4. When you get to Piazza San Felice, turn right onto Via Maggio, which is lined with antiques shops. Take your pick. The word *antichità* refers to antiques in Italian. Poke into R. di Clemente (No. 64), with its big, important pieces of furniture and tapestries; Dinolevi (No. 53r), which specializes in tapestries, antique carpets, and the like; S. Morelli (No. 51), which happens to look like a church inside—very old, handcrafted tables and desks are sold here; Biagiotti Roberta Gravili (No. 49r), which has magnificent

hanging chandeliers (your stewardess will love you for carrying one on board) as well as an eclectic stable of chairs, tables, and paintings; and Artstudio (No. 41r), which carries a little of everything and has a big room in the back with pieces of buildings that can be used as art or made into new furnishings—such as coffee tables.

5. After you get to about No. 27 and until Borgo San Jacopo, the pickings are slim, and what's there is hidden inside old buildings (as at No. 44), but there are many worthwhile shops in here if you like to hunt and explore.

6. Once you get to Via Maggio and Borgo San Jacopo, turn right. Borgo San Jacopo has fewer antiques shops and more restaurants, but can you think of a better combination?

7. Or check out Via Maggio, because it does have some good stores.

8. Finish your tour of the Pitti side of the Arno at Flos, Borgo San Jacopo 62. Flos, as you know, is one of the leading avant-garde design showrooms specializing in lighting. Once you've had a good look at the past, it's always fun to peek into the future. Then cross the river at Ponte Vecchio.

9. Once on the Duomo side of the Arno, turn left and head for Via de' Tornabuoni. At the corner of Via de' Tornabuoni and Lungarno Corsini there are many design and fabrics showrooms; several are branches of famous design studios you have heard about. Look into Techno, Via de' Tornabuoni 5, a big white Memphis-designed showroom with very modern office furniture; Lorenzo Rubelli (No. 3r), wonderful upholstery fabrics, made and stocked locally—they will ship; Cesari (No. 2), equally wonderful upholstery fabrics in prints, stripes, and colors—they, too, will ship;

and Knoll (No. 4), the first—and last—word in office furniture for the home.

10. Begin to wind up your tour by strolling Via de' Tornabuoni and looking into all the shops that interest you. This is the high-rent district where the hoity-toity antiques dealers have taken space alongside the hoity-toity designers of couture and ready-to-wear. There's nothing to complain about in this neighborhood, except maybe the prices. Follow Via de' Tornabuoni to Via della Vigna Nuova and then to Borgo Ognissanti—this will zigzag you to a good resting place and take you by many antiques shops (and fashion shops, too). You'll dead-end at the Grand Hotel, where you can rest your feet and have a lemonade—or something stronger if you need it. You will have seen about two thirds of Florence's antiques shops.

# Day Trip: Pistoia

OK, OK, so you weren't planning on a side trip to Pistoia. In fact, you've never even heard of it and think you can survive without it. Wrong. Pistoia may not be the garden spot of Italy, but it is the home of the **BRUNETTO PRATESI** factory. At the Pratesi factory there is a little shop that sells—you guessed it—seconds. Until now, this shop had been open only to Pratesi employees and friends of the family. But if you show your copy of this book, or say you are a friend of ours, you will be allowed to shop there.

We have heard many and varied reports from people who have gone here; one person complained that the prices were outrageously high; several others wrote us that they were thrilled, that all the sales help spoke English, and that the factory was warm and friendly and quite willing to please. We checked it out recently, through a spy (obviously, Mr. Pratesi knows us, so we can't go sneaking around), who came back with a glowing report. Like all factory outlets, the store sells what it has; you may be lucky or you may not.

Pistoia is not quite an hour away from Florence, and is only about ten minutes from Montecatini Terme, the famous spa area, so you may want to combine both stops on an afternoon jaunt. The scenery on the way to Pistoia is not gorgeous, but you drive on a freeway, so you don't need to worry about country roads. The town of Pistoia itself has a good bit of medieval charm to it, and there's a wonderful country-inn type of family restaurant that we adore—so all in all, you'll have a wonderful time.

Pratesi, as you probably know, is a family business. The current head is Athos Pratesi, whose father, Brunetto, began the business. They make sheets not only for the royalty of Europe and the movie stars of Hollywood, but also for the Pope. Athos, like his father before him, is a stickler for details—a perfectionist. He has a computer that counts the number of stitches in each quilt. If there are five stitches too many, the quilt is a reject! What do they do with this poor, unfortunate, deformed quilt? It will never see the light of day in Beverly Hills, Manhattan, Palm Beach, or even Rome. No, because it has all of five stitches too many, it will be considered a reject, a defect, a second. It will be sold, at a fraction of its *wholesale* price, in the company shop. It's your lucky day.

The store is in the factory, which is a low-lying building, of the modern sort, set off the street on your left as you come off the highway and most noticeable only by the discreet signs that say BRUNETTO PRATESI. We're not talking about the middle of town; this is off a country road. But because it's the most famous factory in the area, everyone does know where it is. Show the printed address to anyone at a nearby gas station or inn and you will get directions. It is not hard. But you are not setting foot into an area that is prepared for tourists.

If all this truly makes you nervous, ask your concierge to call ahead of time and get very specific directions for you, and arrange for a person to call in case you get lost. Also note that the shop is closed during lunch.

A tour of the factory (which has to be arranged privately) will allow you to see the 1,040 separate operations that go into making the average (as if a Pratesi were average) sheet. One iota of a mistake and a black stamp relegates the offender to the seconds shop. This is comforting for two reasons: When you buy Pratesi retail you can be assured of getting the most assiduously pursued quality; and when you shop in the seconds shop, you can find a lot of wonderful things—many with negligible damage. Of the buys in the seconds shop, Athos looks at the item and the price and shakes his head. "It's like making a gift," he says in Italian. Some prices are giftier than others. Not everything here is rock-bottom cheap! Price on an item varies depending on the defect; some items are visibly damaged, some are not. Mr. Pratesi's office sent us a list of notes and guidelines to pass on, so we quote:

Concerning the shop where we sell the defective items:

1. The articles you find in our factory's shop were not accepted by our quality control service.

2. The articles are therefore slightly defective. The defects can be large or small.

3. The articles have to be carefully checked when purchased, since they are neither replaceable nor refundable.

4. The purchased items can not any more be produced.

5. In the event of mailing, the payment should be in advance and mailing charges must be paid by the consignee.

You must pay cash for your purchases, but they will accept dollars. Each item you buy comes with a tag that announces it is damaged, or an "End Collection," as the card says. There is also a smaller tag and maybe a stamp (it will wash out) that says you have bought a damaged piece. Do not think that you can buy a damaged piece and then return it to a Pratesi shop and claim you found a damaged item and try to get money back. Besides being tacky and fraudulent, this ploy will be rejected, since all Pratesi employees know about the maniacal quality control imposed at the factory. It is totally impossible for damaged goods to come into the marketplace.

Hours: Monday, 2 P.M. to 7 P.M.; Tuesday to Friday, 9 A.M. to noon and 2 P.M. to 7 P.M.; Saturday 9 A.M. to 1 P.M.

**BRUNETTO PRATESI, S.p.A.**, Località Ponte Stella, 51034, Pistoia

# Day Trip: Siena

S iena is not very far from Florence, but it takes some thinking about, should you decide to go. The train ride, which is free to you if you have a railroad pass, is very long (over two hours) and often involves changing trains. It's a better use of your time to pay an additional $12–$15 (round trip) and buy a bus ticket. The bus takes an hour and twenty minutes and gives you a very good tour of Florence, as you leave town, and of the hills along the way. You can take a bus from Siena to San Gimignano to see the medieval hillside village (no designer shops!), or you can buy a tour package for the day (from Florence), which will take you to both cities. It's a very pleasant day trip, especially nice for a Monday morning when most of the stores in Florence are closed anyway.

Should you want to stay in Siena, there are many hotels, although we prefer either the out-and-out elegance at the Park Hotel Siena, an old villa on the edge of town that has been converted to a deluxe hotel (it is a CIGA hotel), or the Jolly Hotel, which is right in the middle of town, a stone's throw from where you will get off the bus, right next to the shopping, and leading to all the winding roads you'll want to explore.

**PARK HOTEL SIENA**, Via Marciano 18 (Telephone: 44803)

**JOLLY HOTEL**, Piazza La Lizza (Telephone: 288448)

## Getting There

If you are planning this as a day trip, you will want to consult your hotel concierge or the little guest booklet *Florence Concierge Information*, which lists the bus schedule to and from Siena. There is basically a bus every hour, although peak travel times have several buses. The SITA station has a sign outdoors directing you to where you buy tickets (*biglietteria*), and an information booth outside of the ticket area. You need not stand in line at the information booth to find out where to buy the tickets; just walk into the glassed-in waiting area. Round-trip tickets are discounted slightly. There is a bar, a snack stand, and a magazine stand here, should you need supplies. You must ask which lane your bus will be loading from; there is a large sign high up the wall near the ticket-buying office, or you can ask at the information booth. The bus is clean, modern, and air-conditioned, although it has no bathroom on board. Enter the bus from the rear, where you validate your own ticket by placing it inside the little box and pressing. Wait for the click, then retrieve your ticket. Seats are comfortable, but not padded.

As you approach Siena, the bus may make local stops. Don't panic. Your stop is the end of the line, San Domenico Church, where most of the people on the bus will exit. If you are getting nervous, note that the bus follows the signs toward *Centro* as it keeps moving into Siena.

## Getting Around

When you get off the bus, note the public bathrooms (very clean, pay toilets) and the tourist information office where they sell you a map to the city. If you are standing with your back to the church facing the tourist information office, you'll see that there are two streets to your right. One bears off slightly, the other turns more dramatically and goes down. The high road will take you directly to the Jolly Hotel, just a few steps away. The low road will connect into the main streets of town and eventually take you to the Duomo. We suggest you explore by going out on the high road and returning on the low road. If you are doing this on a Monday morning, most of the stores in Siena are closed—however, if you take the low road, you'll see many touristy stores that are open, even on Monday. They knew you were coming! If you must get a shopping fix immediately, you may want to take this route. Whichever road you take, it's not a bad idea to buy the map.

## Shopping in Siena

The biggest event of the year in Siena is the Palio, a big carnival of a procession in which horsemen rush down the ramps onto the Piazza del Campo while the various flags of the 12th-century gentry flap in the breeze. Once you begin your shopping spree you will notice that replicas of these flags are sold everywhere, especially at the touristy booths along the Campo, and that some of the plates and locally painted faience have designs related to these flags and to symbols that date back to medieval traditions. The Palio, which is actually a horse race, is still run every year, and is one of the most colorful events you will ever see. Pageantry, hoopla, and color are things this city knows a lot about—your shopping opportunities will reflect this flair.

While Siena has branches of the various Italian chains (yes, there's a Benetton everyplace you look), the best buys are on pottery and faience. The designer shops are small, even smaller than in Florence; the selection in other Italian cities is superior. Nevertheless, the shopping here is very seductive and special.

The main shopping street is Via Banchi di Sopra, which leads right to the Campo and then goes up the hill as the Via di Citta. Take this to the cathedral (well marked) and then follow the signs back down and up the Via della Sapienza, which will bring you back to the bus stop at San Domenico. Via della Sapienza has a good number of wine (this is chianti country) and tourist shops, especially close to the bus stop. These remain open during lunchtime, too.

As you approach the Campo, you'll notice various alleys that lead into the square. Some have steps; others are ramps for horses. Each entryway seems to be named for a saint. The Campo is encircled with cafés and shops; many of the alleyways that lead from the shopping street to the Campo are also filled with booths or touristy stands. There are more freestanding booths on the Campo itself.

## Snack and Shop

The Piazza del Campo has many outside cafés where you can eat or snack or watch the world go by. However, we think the best snack in town is sold from a wooden booth in the middle of the square—where you buy a bag of powdered sugar treats called *frittèlle di riso*—fried rice balls.

**NANNINI:** There are a half-dozen Nannini locations along the main walkways of the tourist area of Siena; who knows how many more there are throughout the city. Nannini is a tearoom, a pastry shop, and a candy shop—some locations are more fancy than others. Some have stand-up bars for your snacks, others have sit-down service. The address listed below is the flagship tearoom, the snazziest of several branches.

**NANNINI**, Via Banchi di Sopra 24

▼

**FONTE GAIA:** One of the many cafés right on the Campo, where you can be part of all the action and right in the thick of the shopping. We plopped down here because, of the many attractive places, this one was recommended in an article we had clipped from *Gourmet* magazine.

**FONTE GAIA**, Piazza del Campo 21r

# Pottery and Faience

The Campo is surrounded by shops; many of them specialize in pottery that is handpainted in dusty shades and follows centuries-old patterns. Some of them are even branches of other stores you will find up the hill, closer to the Duomo. The best shops are clustered up the Via di Citta, close to the Duomo—you will automatically pass them as you walk around and up.

**ZINA PROVEDDI:** A cute shop with painted tiles set into wood, it features stacks of plates piled high and giant jars perched on the top shelves. Not every piece is a treasure, but it's a wonderful place to get your introduction to the local pottery works. You'll see many patterns here that will repeat themselves in every shop you visit. After a while, it will be hard to find the pieces that are different—yet each shop does have some items that the neighboring shops don't seem to have. Prices are quite moderate; you can buy just about anything for $15 or $20. The large, impressive pieces are often under $100. You just have to figure out how to get them home.

**ZINA PROVEDDI,** Via di Citta 96

▼

**ARCAICO:** This is our favorite of the local choices, possibly because we love religious pieces, cherubs, and little ceramic holders with madonnas painted on them. This store is by no means a religious shop; it just happens to have a larger percentage of these items than the other shops. You will find the plaster cherubs elsewhere, but we think the selection is best here. You may find prices slightly cheaper in other shops, but for quality and vibrant colors, this is our pick. Cherubs begin at $20; plates and faience items begin around $13; little pitchers are $8. This store also happens to be open on Monday mornings.

**ARCAICO**, Via di Citta 81

▼

**MARTINI MARISA:** These folks have several shops selling pottery and faience and even souvenir items. There are two shops up close to the Duomo, on Via del Capitano (No. 5 and No. 11), and then there is yet another shop down by the Campo. All three have a slightly different feel to them; all have a good selection of basic items.

**MARTINI MARISA**, Via del Capitano 5 and 11
**ANTICA SIENA**, Piazza del Campo 28

▼

**TONINA CANAPINI:** This looks very much like a TT (tourist trap) to us, but that has never stopped us before. No surprise; it is a TT—with a difference. Much of the merchandise here is not seen elsewhere, and a lot of it, despite its touristy nature, is fabulous in style and price. Our best buy was a set of wooden salad servers with molded ceramic handles with handpainted, brightly colored flowers. For $6, these are great gifts. There's also a lot of copper, some ironwork, and a lot of little trinkets. Open Monday and during lunch. We call this a good find. Very close to San Domenico and the bus stop.

**TONINA CANAPINI**, Via della Sapienza 88

## Finds

**MERCATO:** Wednesday is market day in Siena at the Piazza La Lizza, which is directly in front of the Jolly Hotel. Market hours are 8 A.M. to 1 P.M.. Although it's mostly a food affair, it's fun and visually gorgeous.

**WINERIES:** There are many, many wineries in the winding streets. Don't miss the wine tasting in the fortress (Fortezza Medicea, near the bus stop at San Domenico but the other way from the roads into town), or any of the gourmet food and wine shops that dot the shopping areas. Many shops sell six-packs of wine, and four-packs, and gift boxes, and crates. This is chianti country and since you're taking the bus, and not driving, you can drink a free taster's cup in each shop.

**LEGATORIA IL PAPIRO:** This shop at Via di Citta 37 is just one branch of the famous chain of paper stores that are all over Italy and even in the United States. Prices are the same in all Italian cities, but this is one of the most charming stores in Siena, and the old-fashioned charm of the city makes it especially appropriate to be buying something like this here. There is another store in Florence.

**DITTA MAURO VOLPONI:** This small shop at Via Banchi di Sopra 28 reeks of Old World glamour, selling top-of-the-line designer this and that, including Etro and Prada goodies. Note the gold leaf, the old wood, the small touches you never find anymore.

# 8 ▼ ROME (ROMA)

## Welcome to Rome

There are cities that grab at your heart and cities that just don't. Rome is a city that may grab you for its beauty, its antiquities (that's old buildings, not antiques shops), or its traffic, but it does not really grab us for shopping. There is a lot of fine shopping to be done in Rome, don't get us wrong—but we're just not wild about this city. Others may tell you they are afraid to go to Rome these days. Not us. We're just afraid to go during the regular retailing season, when it can be high-priced and boring. Sales time in Rome livens things up considerably. Then you won't catch us complaining too much.

There was a time that Rome was the fashion capital of Italy—but most of the younger, hip designers work from the Milan area. Roman fashion is old couture fashion or English preppy-Italo fashion. Roman fashion is to "do" the Spanish Steps and simply smile.

## Booking Rome/1

If you are driving, or even walking a lot, in Rome you will want a copy of *Rome A to Z,* which is patterned on the London map and city index, with large-size pages in detail. You can buy this paperback book in a bookstore or at any of the several bookstalls on the Via Veneto. You can also buy a city bus map, if you are planning on in-depth exploring. The

*Rome Yellow Pages* is in English and lists everything you need to know and how to get everyone you need to get who speaks English.

There are several good bookstores with English-American books (one of them is across the street from the Grand Hotel), but you'll find the above-mentioned goodies, as well as a huge selection of periodicals from all over the world, guidebooks, American novels, and truly everything you could imagine wanting or needing right at the major newsstands on Via Veneto.

Finally, if you don't want to buy any books on Rome and you aren't anywhere near the Via Veneto, try this: Look for the supplement to the Rome phone books that should be in your hotel room next to the phone books. *Tutta Città* yearly guides are the same size as a phone book, but only a quarter of an inch thick. The title means "All City," and this is truly an all-city guide, with maps, phone numbers, advertising, and all sorts of information. It is all in Italian, but you can figure out a lot of it by yourself.

# Booking Rome/2

Finding a hotel in the middle of the shopping area is not hard—almost every big hotel chain has an entry on the Via Veneto alone. The Hilton is a bit out of town, and the Sheraton is very much out of town (next to the convention area outside of Rome), but you'll have no trouble coordinating your stay with a good shopping location. We rate hotels as inexpensive (under $100 per night), moderate ($100–$150 per night), and expensive (over $150 per night).

**LE GRAND HOTEL:** The most famous hotel in Rome is the Grand, which is conveniently located across from the main train station, at the top of the shopping district. Walk down the hill to get to everything from airline offices to stores to McDonald's. Celebrities wouldn't be caught anywhere else; models and fashion types have English-style high tea here, which is the best buy in Rome, at about $22 per person. A CIGA hotel; expensive. U.S. reservations, (800) 221-2340. The Excelsior, another CIGA hotel which is not as grand as the Grand but which is quite nice, is on the Via Veneto.

LE GRAND HOTEL, Via Vittorio Emanuele Orlando 3 (Telephone: 4709)

EXCELSIOR, Via Veneto 125 (Telephone: 4708)

▼

**JOLLY VIA VENETO:** One of those new-fangled, post–World War II, high-style modern Italian buildings, the Jolly gives you the best of both worlds. Your room overlooks the park and you are situated at the top of the Via Veneto, so you just roll out of bed and into the stores. Moderate to expensive. U.S. reservations, (800) 247-1277.

JOLLY VIA VENETO, Corso Italia 1 (Telephone: 8495)

▼

**D'INGHILTERRA:** Imagine a quaint little English-style hotel that is virtually next door to Valentino—they share a wall. Located at the Spanish Steps, in the midst of the most elegant Roman shopping, this small hotel is a real gem that is often hard to book. They seem to have no U.S. office, which makes it that much more difficult. A hangout for fashion types as well as big names of yesteryear.

Expensive. The bar is open from 11 A.M. to midnight, so stop by or rest up from a shopping spree.

**D'INGHILTERRA**, Via Bocca di Leone 14 (Telephone: 672161)

# Getting There

Y ou can arrive at Rome's airport from anyplace in the world, or come in at the main train station. We've taken the sleeper train from Paris, which gets you into Rome bright and early in the morning, ready to go shopping, as well as local trains. Rome is only two hours from Florence by train, so you could make it a day trip.

# Getting Around

A s you emerge from the main train station, you'll see taxis everywhere; you may even be approached by some drivers who offer their services. Yet there is an official taxi stand with a very long line. You wonder why you don't just hop in one of the waiting cabs, defying the queue. Why are all those people standing in line for up to twenty minutes? Because they don't want to overpay.

Taxi drivers in Rome are known to be difficult, especially to tourists, especially to Americans who can't speak Italian, and most especially to women traveling without men. Be prepared to occasionally have to argue with the driver if you frequent cabs; be aware of when you should pay a supplement (for extra baggage or after 9 P.M. and on Sundays and holidays).

Legitimate taxis are yellow and carry a shield with a number. Cars for hire are black with a shield. Taking any other car can be dangerous. Rome is very spread out; the *metropolitana* is nice, and gets you to all the touristy attractions, but it does not blanket the city. You may find the walk from your hotel to the nearest stop (look for the big red *M* sign) worthy of a taxi in itself. To ride the *metro*, have change to put into the ticket-making machine, or look around for a machine that produces change. You must create your own ticket; there is no booth selling tickets. The newsstand will not give you change without a purchase. Because the *metro* is not too involved, it is easy to ride, and it is relatively safe.

We like to take the bus in Rome, although many people will tell you that they are slow and not dependable, especially in the rain. But the bus gives you a nice view of the gorgeous city, and gets you easily to the main attractions. You can buy a bus map at a newsstand; you can ask your concierge which bus to take; or, you can look at a bus stop and read the sign, which has all the stops listed. We once took the right bus in the wrong direction—a typical mistake for those who don't speak the language or know their way around the city very well—but we had a great time and saw a lot of sights. Rome has many bus islands that act as little stations where buses congregate. There's one such island in front of the Vittorio Emanuele monument in the old city, and another called San Silvestro, which is in the heart of the shopping district at the base of the Via Veneto and halfway to the Spanish Steps.

The bus system in Rome is similar to those in other Italian cities—you should have already purchased your ticket at a tobacco stand or newsstand (they do not sell tickets on the bus or take money); you enter from the rear and cancel your own ticket in the box. Exit from the center of the bus. Instructions in English and Italian are inside the bus.

If you have a little money to spend, you may want a car and driver. The concierge at the Grand got us a driver with a Mercedes to take us to Leonardo da Vinci airport for the same price as a taxi. Ask your concierge about this possibility. We've kept in touch with our original driver, who speaks English, gives you details about the sights you are passing even if you are just going to the airport, and is as handsome as a movie star. He will pick you up at the airport, take you to the airport, or drive you around town for the day or half day. He costs $200–$250 a day (but he goes the whole day, not just eight hours) and is adorable: Sandro Patrizi, Via F. Poggi 52, Roma 00149 (Telephone: 6814787, or car phone: 03/3371737).

## Snack and Shop Rome

**NINO:** Our favorite restaurant in Rome, Nino is where we eat lunch and dinner almost every day we can. A small café with dark wood walls, the restaurant is right in the heart of the shopping in the Spanish Steps and attracts a nice, fashiony crowd without being chichi. Prices are moderate.

**NINO**, Via Borgognona 11 (Telephone: 6795676)

▼

**McDONALD'S:** Stop laughing. We love this McDonald's. And not just for our kids. The architecture (it's in a fake villa) is astounding, the location (Spanish Steps) is sublime, and the food is inexpensive—by Rome, if not by U.S., standards. You can get the usual burgers and McNuggets, but we load up at the salad bar, where we can get tomatoes and mozzarella. You have to see this place and the crowd it gets—it is amazing. Good pit stop to rest between the stores; Logan says to sit downstairs, where it's less noisy.

**McDONALD'S**, Spanish Steps

▼

**DONEY CAFÉ:** This place is a tad expensive for what you get, and there is a high cover charge, but still—if you like sitting in Old World luxury and watching the world go by, you'll want a streetside or window table at Doney on the Via Veneto. You can have a full meal, a snack, or tea. There are other cafés on the Via Veneto, but this is the "in" one. Part of the Excelsior Hotel.

**DONEY CAFÉ**, Via Veneto 125

▼

**RISTORANTE GIRARROSTO TOSCANO:** Possibly better for dinner than lunch, as you will be unable to walk or move after you eat here. We've never seen so much food in our lives. This country style eatery is at the top of the Via Veneto (across the street from the Jolly, around the corner from the Excelsior); sit down and they automatically start bringing food. This is the *antipasto*, for which there is a flat charge per person, no matter how much you eat. After you've eaten more than you knew possible, they bring the menu, and you can eat more. Moderate to expensive. Closed Wednesdays. (Telephone: 4463759)

**RISTORANTE GIRARROSTO TOSCANO**, Via Campania 29

## Best Buys of Rome

This is a short section. There aren't any best buys.

Rome is gorgeous, but it really isn't a great city for shopping. Yes, yes, all the stores are here and you'll have no trouble finding boutiques and fashion feasts for the eyes, but the best selection is in Milan and the best buys are in Florence.

If you are bargain-conscious, the best deals in Rome are at a few outlet shops (page 216) or in the airport, which has a gigantic duty-free shopping area at which everything is discounted 18%. Please note that the items imported to Italy (English sweaters, for example) are 18% cheaper than they are in a regular Italian store—but they are still outrageously expensive. Buy Italian when in Italy, and don't be shy about that airport shopping center. The Trussardi canvas duffel bag cost $150 in the Trussardi shop at the Spanish Steps, and $130 in the airport. The duty-free also sells Chanel and Hermès scarves at discount. This is cheaper than you will find them in the Chanel or Hermès shops in Paris, unless you spend enough to qualify for the *détaxe* there.

## Hours

Hours in Rome are the same as in all of Italy. Ask your concierge about saints' days and holidays. Most shops open at 9:30 A.M. and close at 1 or 1:30 P.M. for lunch. They reopen at 3:30 in winter and at 4:00 in summer. In the summer, stores stay open until 8 P.M. Because Romans (as do all Europeans) dine late, many people are out shopping and window-shopping until midnight. We stick to the heavily trafficked areas after dark, but you'll have no trouble finding crowded streets at almost any time of the year. In winter stores close Monday morning; in summer, Saturday afternoon.

If you don't like to give up shopping for lunch, the department stores and mass merchandisers stay open during these hours, while a growing number of high-end merchants are following suit. Fendi is open through lunch, as are other stores on Via Borgognona.

# Neighborhoods

## Spanish Steps

No matter what season of the year, the Spanish Steps are so gorgeous that you can't help but be drawn to them. They are particularly magical to us because they lead to all our favorite stores. And on the way, we pass all those street merchants who cluster around the Steps waiting for tourists to come buy their wares. For a blow-by-blow of the area, see page 218. Don't forget that there's an American Express office here—so when you run out of money on a shopping spree, you can get more money without missing a beat, and then get right back to spending it.

## Trevi

From the Spanish Steps you can walk to the Fountain of Trevi (don't forget to visit our favorite shop for Fila [Giusti] while you're there) and segue into several "real people"

# Rome

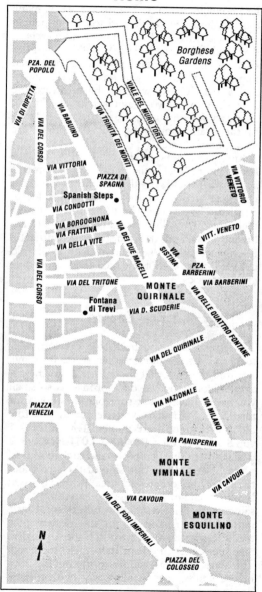

Rome neighborhoods. You won't see as many tourists, and you won't find too many people who speak English, but you will find merchandise and fair prices. Hit Via Tritone—both sides of the street have good offerings; then there's Via Nazionale, which is a cab ride away, and Via del Corso, which is back toward the Spanish Steps. If you can't get to all of these areas, try for one or two. They're not as fancy as the grand boutiques, but the prices are much, much better.

Right at the Fountain of Trevi is a large sports store that sells men's and women's active wear—**GIUSTI**—that is one of the most complete sources in Italy. They sell a lot of American sportswear, and the prices are so high they are silly, so watch what you are buying. Check out the side streets around here, if only to look. Via del Lavatore is an old cobbled street with a few nice shops and some cheap eateries.

## Via dei Coronari

This street takes you back to a previous century, and has the best antiques stores in Rome. Located right around the corner from the Piazza Navona, the Via dei Coronari is so small you might have to ask someone or study your map first. Start at Navona, enter this narrow old back street, and immediately at No. 1 you'll hit pay dirt: **ROMANO LOTT-MARA** is a dealer in antique sculpture and archaeological pieces. Walk down one side of the street and back up the other—an area of maybe two blocks. Some of the shops are extremely fancy salons with priceless pieces, others are a little more funky. Almost all of the dealers take credit cards; those who don't speak English may speak French if your Italian isn't too good. The shop numbers will go to the middle 200s before you've seen it all, easily two or three dozen prime shops.

## Via del Corso

Via del Corso is a very long street; the part that you will be most interested in begins where Via del Tritone intersects it, and all of Via del Corso from there to Piazza del Popolo is a very nice walk. Both sides of the street are lined with stores—many are branches of famous names, such as **FRETTE, FIORUCCI,** or even **BENETTON,** and many are stores that we are just attracted to, such as **LINEASPORT** (No. 49), where we buy Fila and sports gear for our husbands and sons. The numbers drop so that No. 49 is closer to the Popolo part. Some other favorites:

**QUEEN BABY:** A children's store, for children and mothers who like wild and imaginative clothes.

**QUEEN BABY,** Via del Corso 80

▼

**CHILDREN'S CLUB:** This is right off Via del Corso, and we thought it was a great place when we found it. Then Logan told us it was one of her secret finds. So there you go. More for locals than for tourists, but still a good resource if your child needs traditional English clothes made out of the finest materials but at affordable prices. Navy blazers and plaid skirts, but the best-made goods at the best prices in Rome.

**CHILDREN'S CLUB,** Via Vittoria 27

## Via Nazionale

Stretching from the train station right into town, the Via Nazionale is a main shopping drag. But the nicer stores are clustered up at the top, near the station and the Piazza della Repubblica.

**FIORUCCI:** Another trendy boutique, whose items we have here in the United States. We found all the glitter and neon accessories that our kids asked us to bring back for them.

FIORUCCI, Via Nazionale 236

▼

**LELLO DEL ARRICCIA:** If you are looking for some extra pieces of china or everyday dinnerware, make it a point to stop by this liquidation shop for silver or china. This very tiny, crowded shop is full of china and crystal from both high-end and inexpensive manufacturers, but sift through the junk—you'll find some good pieces. We uncovered good prices on Richard Ginori's dishes.

LELLO DEL ARRICCIA, Via Nazionale 238

▼

**PUER:** If you've drooled for designer clothes but haven't had the heart or the money to go through with your fantasy, then stop by this rather large shop and feast your eyes on their selection of designer copies. We find their casual clothes to be of better quality than their dressier items.

PUER, Via Nazionale 232

▼

**ALEXIA:** This is a wonderful shop filled with a large assortment of designer handbags, suitcases, wallets, briefcases, shoes, and leather coats. There are three large, well-stocked rooms filled with a multitude of items at very good prices. Designers such as Ungaro, Emilio Pucci, Enrico Coveri, YSL, and Fila are represented.

**ALEXIA**, Via Nazionale 242

▼

**FRETTE:** Now is the time to indulge in buying those lovely bed ensembles you've always wanted. A beautiful king-size peach and white appliquéd quilt with a matching set of sheets and pillow covers is $420, although you can find a simple quilt for $95. If you feel that you've neglected your bathroom, you can find lovely appliquéd sets costing $100, with a matching terry bathrobe for yourself at $70.

**FRETTE**
Via Nazionale 84
Via del Corso 381

## Via del Tritone

This is a big shopping street that connects the Via del Corso and Spanish Steps area to the Via Veneto and Piazza Barberini area. At the top is the Piazza Barberini, with the Bernini Bristol Hotel and a *metro* stop. As you move down the street until it dead-ends into Via del Corso, you have a lot of "real people" shops with more moderate prices. There's also the San Silvestro bus station at the Piazza San Silvestro. There is a large La Rinascente department store on the corner. If you walk a few blocks away from the Spanish Steps, you'll be at the Fountain of Trevi. Should you happen to want to mail a package, send it Express Mail from the main post office right at Piazza San Silvestro. As a connector, Via del Tritone offers you the way to many places: Use it to get to San Silvestro to take a bus anywhere or cut over on the Via dei Due Macelli to the Spanish Steps, or go the full distance to the Via del Corso and then turn right and head for the streets that fan off the Spanish Steps. There are a few good bookstores on Via del Tritone, as well as the usual Benettons, and a few other finds.

**REIS:** A large specialty store, Reis sells all the licensed Valentino lines. We found a black short cocktail dress with rhinestone bow for about $375 that we still can't believe we didn't buy. We saw it again in Paris for $100 more and then couldn't buy because we could have (should have!) bought it in Rome. The help does not speak English; tourists rarely come here, but you'll find a lot to choose from at possibly the best retail prices in town. If you want to impress your friends with a Valentino label but can't hack the couture prices (who can?), you can get yourself a very wonderful outfit here.

**REIS**, Via del Tritone 128–31

▼

**SERMONETA:** If you love lace tablecloths and whitework on linen, stop by Sermoneta for many handmade items. They also have infant sweaters identical to ones we've seen in the windows at Pratesi. They take plastic and will ship anywhere in the world. This is a mom-and-pop operation, and the people are lovely. If you buy $100 wedding presents for your loved ones, you can do very nicely here. It's not Pratesi by any means, but if traditional whitework is your thing, there's lots to love here.

**SERMONETA**, Via del Tritone 168

▼

**UPIM:** A fancy dime store that's a good resource for cheap gifts, kids' clothes, and whatnots. They're also open during lunch.

**UPIM**, Via del Tritone 172

## Via del Babuino

This is one of the antiques neighborhoods of Rome, where some of the snazziest shops can be found. It is a fun neighborhood, especially if you're just looking—for furniture, paintings, or the hottest items in Europe these days, Art Deco tabletop accessories. This street stretches from the Spanish Steps to Piazza del Popolo, and is filled with interior-design experts, antiques shops, and fabric and lighting showrooms.

## The Grand

While the Grand Hotel is not surrounded by shops, there are two or three directly across the street that make it all worthwhile:

**FELTRINELLI:** A large and well-stocked bookstore with titles in every language, including Russian. Excellent travel section; good selection of American and English books.

FELTRINELLI, Via Vittorio Emanuele Orlando 90

▼

**ESTIVI:** One of the best perfume shops in Rome, with a huge selection of fake jewels, makeup and beauty treatments, and all sorts of hair clips and fun goodies. We could spend hours here, and millions . . . of *lire*. The prices are very high, but the selection and ambience are superlative.

ESTIVI, Via Vittorio Emanuele Orlando 92

## The Ghetto

This is a far cry from the Grand Hotel, but for those of you who want to stay in a fabulous hotel but then travel to the grittier parts of the city, you are off on a crazy adventure. Take a bus from the train station to the Vittorio Emanuele monument and walk, or just taxi, right to the oldest part of Rome, where the ghetto was. Take the Via delle Botteghe Oscure for two short blocks, note all the fabric jobbers, then turn left at the Piazza Paganica. You'll now enter a small neighborhood that seems very residential. Wander the weaving streets looking for the shops that interest you. This is the kind of adventure that is welcomed by a true garmento, someone who likes to see bolts of fabric piled up in store windows and doesn't care about fancy architecture or salesgirls in matching uniforms. The area is charming—very old and crumbling and undiscovered by tourists. All of these stores are jobbers; you'll find jeans and underwear and sweats and even a few jewelry stores. Our favorite finds:

**ZARFATI:** For perfumes that are closer to duty-free prices, rather than outrageous Roman prices, you can buy from this spare little supplier who has all the big names in Italian designer perfume, from Gucci to Missoni to Ferré. There are a few French and American brands, also. Prices are 30% off regular retail.

ZARFATI, Via Falegnami 7–9

▼

**LEONE LIMENTANI:** You asked for it, you got it: the place where locals go for discounted china from the big names, such as Richard Ginori and Villeroy & Boch and even Royal Doulton. This is actually a hotel-supply jobber, with stock in room after dusty room. If you like this sort of thing, this is heaven. In business since 1820, the store handles brides and wedding lists and locals who know where to get the best deals in Rome.

**LEONE LIMENTANI**, Via Portico d'Ottavia 47

## Via Veneto

The Via Veneto was the fanciest shopping and strolling street in Rome after World War II. It still has some faded elegance, but no longer competes with the Spanish Steps area. If your hotel is nearby, you may want to browse. The bookstalls are fabulous; the cafés are great. (Doney is closed on Mondays.) There are a few fabulous stores.

**ELIZA:** This is one of the jazziest stores in Rome, and could lead the way in bringing the Via Veneto back to its former position as a place of high concepts and styles. Eliza feels as swanky as any atelier in Paris. The clothes are very expensive and come from the biggest names in Italian and American fashion. They even carry Norma Kamali here. This is a very intimate, chic store where you can trust the salespeople to make you over for your Roman holiday. One store is classic, the other young and kicky.

**ELIZA**, Via Veneto 157 and 192

▼

**RAPHAEL SALATO:** This is really Raphael's street—his sense of style keeps the block breathing. He has several shoe stores, including one that sells incredible children's shoes. There is a nice store at the Spanish Steps, but these

stores are less crowded. Shoes begin around
$100 and go up and up and up.

**RAPHAEL SALATO**, Via Veneto 104 and 149

▼

**ALBANESE:** This shoe store is a good find,
since they make shoes that resemble Andrea
Pfister styles, but sell them for less than half
the Pfister price. You can do very well here in
the $150–$200 range, which only buys you
one shoe in many stores. A good find.

**ALBANESE**, Via Veneto 183

▼

**EXCLUSIVE:** A tiny shoe shop for kids,
where you can get Gucci loafers or silver
woven leather flats (only $100) and all sorts of
high-fashion shoes just like Mom's and Dad's,
but for the little ones. There are Valentino
shoes for Mom, starting at $200.

**EXCLUSIVE**, Via Veneto 124

▼

**BRUNO MAGLI:** We were shocked to discover that prices on Magli shoes go up after
you reach size 40 (U.S. size 9), so that the
prices in the window for the shoes we wanted
were not the real prices for those who have big
feet. This is not a very glamorous store, but if
you insist on Magli, you can stock up here,
right at the edge of the Via Veneto.

**BRUNO MAGLI**, Via Veneto 70

# Continental Big Names

I t's always nice to visit the Continental big-name stores in any city in the world. It is especially interesting to do so in Italy, because many French designers (like Ungaro) manufacture their clothes in Italy, so you can find prices competitive with those in France. Except for Céline, most of these French designers have very small shops. Some have picked up and left—like Givenchy. Very few new ones arrive; the trend here is for Italian design, or for a specialty store to stock other designers:

**CACHAREL,** Via del Gambero 18
**CARTIER,** Via Condotti 83
**CÉLINE,** Via Borgognona 4
**FOGAL,** Via Condotti 55
**MAUD FRIZON,** Via Borgognona 38
**HERMÈS,** Via Condotti 60
**KENZO,** Via Babuino 124A
**UNGARO,** Via Bocca di Leone 24

# Italian Big Names

**GIORGIO ARMANI:** There are two shops—men's and women's; they are not huge and not very dramatic when compared to the Milan shop, but they do have everything you might need to dress you and your man in head-to-toe Armani at prices about 30% cheaper than in the United States. Don't be surprised if you bump into a few American celebs here.

**GIORGIO ARMANI,** Via del Babuino 102
**EMPORIO ARMANI,** Via del Babuino 140

**BATTISTONI:** For many years, Battistoni has been the most fashionable tailor in Rome. It is also the Rome outlet for Chanel. Signore Battistoni began his career over forty years ago as a small shirtmaker. By the 1950s he had become both popular and famous. The shop on Via Condotti is his most central location, carrying not only the Chanel clothing (upstairs), but also Battistoni's own line of leathergoods and clothes. The shop is tiny and always seems to be crowded with Italian women buying anything and everything, including the classic Chanel suit. The Battistoni tailor shop is tucked away behind the main shop in a courtyard at Nos. 60–61. Here you can order bespoke suits and shirts.

**BATTISTONI**
 Via Condotti 57 (women)
 Via Condotti 60–61 (men)

▼

**BENETTON:** Right at the Spanish Steps you'll find one of Italy's most common national treasures—another Benetton shop. In the same area are other similar shops, such as Sisley, etc.

**BENETTON**, Piazza di Spagna, 94–95
**012**, Via Frattina 1
**BENETTON/012**, Via Condotti 89
**SISLEY**, Via Condotti 196

▼

**CUCCI:** No, that's not a typographical error. There really is a Cucci, and they are no relation to Gucci! Cucci is the Brooks Brothers of Italy. A family firm with a fine reputation for quality, and one that sells to many stars, Cucci is famous for their finely tailored suits and elegant sportswear. We find the shop very sterile and the fashions rather boring. However, with their success they must be doing something right!

CUCCI
Via Condotti 67
Cavalieri Hilton

▼

**FENDI:** A visit to any of the Fendi shops in Rome can only be described as a religious experience. The big main shop is mind-boggling. There are a couple of little stores; the main store goes all the way through the block, so it has an entrance on either side. Young, with-it, and oh-so-chic, Fendi has something for everyone at prices that are amazingly affordable. The business has grown into a $200-million-a-year family jackpot that is run by the five Fendi sisters, who all live in Rome. Each one has a specialty—Paola is said to be the queen of the Russian fur market for all the pelts she has bought for the famous Fendi furs (designed by Karl Lagerfeld, natch). Each Fendi purchase comes in a beautiful lacquered bag that assures the honoree you have not purchased a copy from the market.

FENDI, Via Borgognona 36, 39, and 40

▼

**SALVATORE FERRAGAMO:** Aside from the Florence shop, all Ferragamo boutiques are like this one—complete, expensive, and impressive. In Rome there are actually two shops very close to each other, one for women's clothing and one for men's. The interiors are very clean and inviting, and done in beige marble and burgundy lacquer. The clothes are drop-dead classic chic at very high prices. Shoe prices may be the same as at home, unless you hit a sale.

SALVATORE FERRAGAMO
Via Condotti 73–74 (women)
Via Condotti 66 (men)

**GUCCI:** Expect Gucci to be mobbed and the sales help to treat you in the inimitable Gucci manner. The good news, however, is that many, many Gucci items are not very expensive. Traditional gift items—key chains, small leathergoods, and tote bags—are so reasonable that you may not even be tempted to buy imitation. And the Gucci gift wrap is exquisite.

Upstairs at Gucci are shoes and clothes as well as luggage and attaché cases; downstairs, the leathergoods and small gifty items.

**GUCCI**
Via Condotti 8 (main store)
Via Condotti 76 (clothes)

▼

**KRIZIA:** The Krizia boutique is next door to the Missoni men's shop, and is almost as tiny. Sweaters start at $300. Prices go up and up. In fact, most prices are shocking.

**KRIZIA,** Piazza di Spagna 77

▼

**MAX MARA:** There is a Max Mara shop in every Italian city you visit, and no doubt you've already discovered what we consider to be the best casual Italian ready-to-wear at its many divisions, including SportMax and Penny Black. Max Mara clothes are not inexpensive, but they cost about 30% less in Italy than in the U.S., and make a fine investment in classic dressing.

**MAX MARA**
Via del Tritone 137
Via Condotti 46
Via Frattina 28

▼

**MISSONI:** The Missoni menswear shop is not near the women's wear shop, and there seems little relationship between the two. We've even heard that they are owned not by the Missonis but by the sister of another famous Italian designer. Well, it takes a good eye to know good stuff.

The Missoni Uomo shop—actually named Uomo 78—is as tiny as a closet. The help is not particularly friendly, and the prices are outrageous. The gorgeous, colorful Missoni knits start at $500 and go up.

The Missoni women's boutique is new and snazzy. They have a good selection of the latest fashions. Prices are equal to those in Milan—about 20% cheaper than in the United States. We like this shop better than the one in Milan; you don't have to worry about breaking your neck going up a darkened stairway to heaven.

MISSONI, Via del Babuino 96a (women)
UOMO 78, Piazza di Spagna 78 (men)

▼

**PRATESI:** If you keep track of Pratesi stores as we do, then you may suspect that somehow Frette has bought out Pratesi. Not so. Frette did buy up many locations where Pratesi franchise stores once stood, but Pratesi has their own new, family-owned stores popping up all over Italy. Their flagship is in Rome, at the top of Via Condotti. We're big on the factory outlet near Florence, but this luxe shop with its timelessly elegant bed fashions is worth swooning over.

PRATESI, Piazza di Spagna 77

▼

**RAPHAEL SALATO:** Raphael Salato has three boutiques on Via Veneto and one on Piazza di Spagna. This is where you will find Andrea Pfister shoes, handbags, and boots in styles so wonderful and artistic that your pocketbook may lose a few pounds (or *lire*). Raphael also has his own equally wonderful line of shoes and boots, as well as a very classic line of shoes for children. The third shop on Via Veneto is a children's shop.

**RAPHAEL JUNIOR**, Via Veneto 96a
**RAPHAEL**, Via Veneto 104
**RAPHAEL SALATO**
 Via Veneto 149
 Piazza di Spagna 34

▼

**VALENTINO:** Ah, Valentino—how we adore you. And how we adore to buy your clothes in Italy, where we can begin to think we can afford them.

While many shops look like converted *palazzi* (and are), Valentino's still looks like a *palazzo*. Inside, the decor is equally dramatic, with white tile floors and black lacquer showcases. The main boutique, however, does not carry a large selection of licensed items—you will find them in the new line "Oliver," named for Valentino's dog.

**VALENTINO**, Via Bocca di Leone 15–18
**OLIVER**, Via del Babuino 61

▼

**MARIO VALENTINO:** This is a tiny shop with some good selections from the Mario Valentino men's and women's collections. A pair of beautiful dress shoes cost upwards of $200. The big store is at the corner of Via del Corso.

**MARIO VALENTINO**, Via Frattina 58 and 84

# Shoes and Leathergoods

There are scads of little shops selling leathergoods all over Rome—and every other major Italian city, for that matter. We've weeded them down to a few special shops—some we like for their elegance, others for their bargains. For the most part, we do our serious leathergoods shopping at Vogini in Venice or at Athos in Florence, but ever since Bottega opened its own shop in Rome, we've come to like shopping here even more than before.

**BOTTEGA VENETA:** This gorgeous Bottega shop is near the Spanish Steps and is hard to find unless you know where to look. Prices are less than in the United States, but there are no bargains here.

BOTTEGA VENETA, Salita San Sebastianello 16b

▼

**TRUSSARDI:** The master of Louis Vuitton chic in his very own style. We like the canvas bags and totes in navy blue with the royal blue contrast trim. Prices for ready-to-wear are too high for us, but the quality is *magnifico*. The airport shop offers a discount on these goods.

TRUSSARDI, Via Bocca di Leone 27

▼

**CAMPANILE SPATARELLA:** This wonderful shop, with its angular black granite entrance, houses four floors of rather expensive but gorgeous Italian leathergoods and clothing. We found browsing through their selection of leather shoes, boots, jackets, and knitted sweaters with leather and rhinestone insets a pleasure—and sometimes a bargain as well. Goods for both men and women.

**CAMPANILE SPATARELLA**, Via Condotti 58

▼

**FAUSTO SANTINI:** If we write home about just one shoe store, it's not Maud and it's not Beltrami, it's the fun and fantasy of the Fausto Santini stores (which are all over Italy and even on Madison Avenue in New York City), with their rainbow-striped tiled storefront. The prices are low and the shoes are wild and crazy.

**FAUSTO SANTINI**, Via Frattina 120

▼

**GUIDO PASQUALI:** Don't turn your nose up at this tiny little shop! Inside, there's a selection of very beautiful and well-made shoes and handbags. Plain pumps start at $75; a small glittered clutch purse is $70.

**GUIDO PASQUALI**, Via Bocca di Leone 5

▼

**DIEGO DELLA VALLE:** This Italian shoe maven is making inroads on fame in the U.S. If you haven't already heard of him, not to worry. Just trot in and head for the Tod's line—a hot Italian yuppie item in sport and driving shoes. Then you'll be the first on your block at home to be an Italian yuppie. Some models of the driving shoes have wraparound rubber soles. There are also more serious styles in men's and women's shoes; very "in." Soon to be a major force in the U.S. Watch this space.

**DIEGO DELLA VALLE**, Via Borgognona 45

# Children's Clothes

I n Italian culture, no one is more precious than the children. As a result, you'll find unbelievably wonderful kids' clothing all over Italy, especially in Rome. Ask to see the Pratesi Baby and the Krizia Baby when you are in these boutiques.

**LA CICOGNA:** Although there's a London branch, do check out the famous flagship store, one of nine stores in Rome and probably the easiest to find. This is where you will fulfill your fantasies of how your children should look if they would only wear the clothes! They carry all the major designer lines for both boys and girls. You can buy your maternity clothes, layette for the new baby, his or her furniture, and everything he or she will need for ages up to fourteen. The decor is plain but elegant, with gray paint and mirrors. The sales help is very friendly and will take you around the store to help you find what you need.

**LA CICOGNA,** Via Frattina 38

▼

**BENETTON / 012:** Search no farther—this is the shop your kids have been longing for. Although the shops often differ, this one is well-stocked, with a collection of pants, sweaters, and shirts. The prices at J.C. Penney's back home are a lot better, but this is what the kids are begging for. Make their dreams come true, Mommy.

**BENETTON / 012,** Via Frattina 45

▼

**FIORUCCI:** If your child is over three, she's probably begging for something punk. You can find a lot of silly gift items and some ready-to-wear at Fiorucci, who invented the wild and wacky stuff we're all finally getting used to. If you're the type who stocks up on gift items for all the birthday parties your kids will be invited to, you can find numerous $5–$10 treasures here—in neon colors, but of course.

FIORUCCI, Via Nazionale 236

# Sporting Goods

I n our never-ending quest for the world's cheapest Fila, we continually prowl the sporting-goods shops of the world, trying to better the prices found in the Rome airport or on Capri. So far, no such luck. But if you can't wait for the airport, not to worry. We have a one-stop that's worth it all, and it's right near the Fountain of Trevi.

**GIUSTI:** Almost three coins' throw from the fountain (it couldn't be more convenient), this large shop once was a private home. The kitchen now is the ski center (downstairs), the main drawing room has women's tennis clothes, etc. You just parade all through the house. Up the winding staircase is the riding department, also the home of those corduroy Fila trousers we have yet to find anyplace else in the world except Beverly Hills. Giusti also stocks Ellesse and other major brands; in fact, they even have some American brands that are very expensive.

GIUSTI, Piazza Trevi

**JACQUES SIMENON:** Knowing the American craze for Fila, Jacques Simenon advertises itself as the center for Fila goods in Rome. We've been unimpressed with the selection after comparing it to that at Giusti. Prices are higher at Simenon, but they do have a pretty good selection, and may have an item Giusti doesn't have.

JACQUES SIMENON
   Via del Corso 150
   Via del Tritone 124

# China and Crystal

**RICHARD GINORI:** If you own Richard Ginori china and have been waiting for your trip to Rome to fill out your set, you won't be disappointed. This is our favorite Ginori in Italy. Although the shop is smallish, it is well-stocked, with all our favorite Ginori patterns and accessories. The sales help is extremely friendly (not at all like those in Milan), and gladly ships.

RICHARD GINORI, Via Condotti 87

▼

**STILVETRO:** If you feel you must come away with a deal, make it a point to stop at this bargain hunter's paradise. Here we found inexpensive Italian china and glassware sets in a variety of styles. There's a lot of junk here, but if you've got what Mother used to call "a good eye," you can find a few treasures that may even be worth shipping home.

STILVETRO, Via Frattina 55

# Fun Jewelry

**CASTELLI:** Ever since we stopped at this strange little shop with costume jewelry in the window and found selections of Christian Dior and Givenchy, we've been hooked, and we have been returning ever since. There's also Castelli's own brand. This small, wood-paneled shop is crammed with perfume, beauty supplies, and their wonderful collection of costume jewelry. Don't miss the variety of evening bags.

**CASTELLI**, Via Condotti 54 and 61

▼

**GABRIELLA FILATI:** Just off Via Condotti, in a shop the size of a closet, we found a wonderful selection of "glitter" and Art Deco pieces. We go there almost every day when we are in Rome, just because we realize we didn't buy enough. *Warning:* Almost everything we buy here breaks easily—know where your nearest hobby or craft shop is so you can make at-home repairs once back in the United States without tearing your hair out.

**GABRIELLA FILATI**, Via Belsiana 70b

▼

**CONSUELO BOZART:** One can leave with a collection of fake Art Deco and other costume jewelry. The styles and selection are great, and they're definitely worth the stop if you didn't get what you wanted in Florence.

**CONSUELO BOZART**, Via Bocca di Leone 4

# Fabrics

**N**ever underestimate the power of a naked seam or your own ability to do it yourself. Rome has one don't-miss-it-shop if you're a home sewer, and several others that offer good buys, especially in designer fabrics.

**POLIDORI:** If you would rather make it yourself, then stop by this smallish shop and pick up your own Italian designer silks and woolens. Also available are a few French fabrics.

**POLIDORI**
  Via Condotti 21a
  Via Borgognona 4a

▼

**CASTELLANO:** If you like your designer fabrics sold in a shop as fancy as the designer's own boutiques, stop by Castellano, which advertises grand-class fabrics on their card. They have all the Valentino fabrics—about $45 a meter. The sales help can be aloof, but warm up if you show you are a spender.

**CASTELLANO**, Via Condotti 37

▼

**BISES:** The best, by far, is the famous Bises, which sells a little of everything in its converted-*palazzo* headquarters. You can get Liberty of London fabric by the meter, as well as every big designer (French and Italian) you can name—right off the bolt. There's also a little bit of ready-to-wear—gorgeous silk blouses made in a rainbow of colors are sold in the

silk department. The knitting yarn department
is fabulous. Don't forget to look up at the
ceiling while you are shopping—all the original frescoes are still there. They have a rather
strange system when it's time to pay. You give
your selections to the clerk and go downstairs
to the ground floor to the cashier and pay
(they take plastic). Your purchase comes down
on a dumbwaiter and is retrieved after you
have paid for it.

**BISES**, Corso Vittorio 1–5

# Papal Shopping

I f you are in quest of religious items (non-
antique varieties), a dozen shops surrounding St. Peter's Square offer everything you've
been looking for. Most of the shops will
send out your purchase to be blessed by the
Pope. Allow twenty-four hours for this service.
Some of the stores will deliver the items—after
the blessing—to your hotel; others ask you to
return for them. If you are having items blessed,
make it clear how you will be getting your
merchandise back. We must say that for the
devout, an item blessed by the Pope makes an
excellent gift.

# Special Events

I f you happen to be in Rome between December 15 and January 6, get yourself (and
your kids) over to the Piazza Navona, where
there is an annual Christmas fair. The stalls
surround the large square and offer food, candies, and crafts. You can buy tree ornaments

and crèches as well as handknit clothes for Cabbage Patch and Passport (the Italian equivalent of Cabbage Patch) dolls. *Warning:* Much of the Hong Kong–made merchandise is less expensive in the United States. We bought a Taiwanese "dynobot" for $15 at the festival and found it for $9 at California's Rose Bowl Swap Meet. The same "dynobot" was $17 in regular toy shops in Rome. Stick to locally crafted items at the fair and you won't get ripped off. We haven't had much luck bargaining here, but you can try.

# Flea Markets and Junk Shops

If you like used merchandise, you might want to poke around **MONTE DI PIETA** at Piazza Pietà. This is a pawnshop where thousands of people go to borrow money against their prized possessions. Over 90% of the items are redeemed, and we hate to send people there to prey on others' hard times— but if this is your kind of thing, you'll never get over this place.

We happen to prefer flea markets, of which there are plenty in Rome. The most famous is held on Sunday from 6 A.M. to 2 P.M. You can get there at 8 A.M. and do fine; this is not like the Bermondsey Market in London, where you must be there in the dark with a flashlight in your hand. In fact, in Rome, we suggest you go to flea markets only in daylight. The big flea market is officially called the **MERCATO DI PORTA PORTESE**—it stretches for about a mile along the Tiber River, where about a thousand vendors are selling everything imaginable—a lot of which is fake or hot (or both). Enter the market about halfway down Viale Trastevere, where the old clothes are. This way you avoid miles of auto accessories.

**VIA SANNIO** is a busy "real people" market area with all kinds of fabulous junk. Everything is cheap in price and quality—this is "less than K mart" time. Many of the vendors who sell on Sunday at Porta Portese end up here during the week, so if you miss Sunday in Rome, don't fret. Just c'mon over here. The crime problem (pickpockets) seems to be less during the week, also. There's a Coin department store on the corner. Come by bus or *metro*.

**PIAZZA VITTORIO EMANUELE** is our favorite Roman market. This market is open every day but Sunday, and is great for tourists who are not that into shopping, since they'll be in this neighborhood anyway. There's food on the northern side and clothes on the southern side. Lots of the clothing and leathergoods are junky, but it's fun to look at it all. If you have teens, you may want to bring them; you can also get some inexpensive gifts here.

**PIAZZA FONTANELLA BORGHESE,** not far from the Spanish Steps, has twenty-four stalls selling prints, maps, books, coins, and some antiques. Open every day nonstop, Monday through Saturday, 9 A.M.–6 P.M., possibly later on summer evenings.

# Bargain Basements

**MAS:** You have to like dives to be able to handle this, but if you're the type of person who thinks shopping heaven is on Manhattan's Lower East Side, you will have no trouble at either of the two Mas stores at Piazza Vittorio. One shop is devoted to furs and leathergoods. Across the street is the ready-to-wear and housewares division—many of the Anglo-Saxon–styled goods are sold here, with or without labels. A Duke of Kent–brand cashmere V-neck sweater is $50. That is the cheapest cashmere sweater you'll find just about anywhere. Bassetti linens, a famous name in beds, makes matrimonial sets for wedding gifts that are divine—white with lace and looking like they were made in the convent—for $40, and that's for four pieces! This is a very low-end store that will turn off all but devoted junksters.

**MAS**, Piazza Vittorio Emanuele

▼

**BALLOON:** Founded in Rome, and with several locations in the suburbs (they don't get too many tourists), Balloon has branched to other Italian cities and is becoming the private-label Loehmann's of its generation. The trick here is that the merchandise is very normal, wearable, and simple—it just has better prices than regular Italian fashion because it is made in China. You'll find mostly sweaters, but there are simple blouses and shirtdresses, etc. You can get basic wardrobe pieces at reasonable prices. Closed Saturday afternoons.

**BALLOON**
  Via della Cafferella 13
  Via Flaminia Vecchia 495
  Piazza di Spagna 35

▼

**ANTICOLI GLOVES FACTORY:** Now for an upscale bargain basement with a tale of caution. We see no reason to believe there is a factory anywhere near this outlet, but it's so conveniently located (a block from the Spanish Steps) that we always make a point to stop here. It's also a place for cheapo gift items. And they will send you a color catalogue and you can mail-order. Gloves, wallets, purses (those little coin purses for tourists), ties, and scarves all are available here—many sold from bins. It's not fancy, but it's kind of fun, *and* they don't close for lunch!

**ANTICOLI GLOVES FACTORY**, Piazza Migna-nelli 22

▼

**SPANISH STEPS:** Yes, one of our favorite bargain basements is not a shop at all but the actual Spanish Steps. Depending on the weather, the number of tourists, and the police, vendors will walk up and down the Steps (they have very strong legs) and sell all kinds of bargains—most of them fake or hot. The police do chase them away from time to time. Look for some of these vendors around Valentino as well. If you can't make it to one of Rome's markets, and if Gucci or Louis Vuitton is too *cara* for you for real, get your bargains here. The best time of day is late afternoon to early evening.

# Rome on a Schedule

## Roman Holiday

Knowing your way around Rome is great; browsing all the stores between the Grand Hotel and the Piazza Navona is fun. But let's get small. The best shopping in Rome is in the Spanish Steps area, and what you really need is a good understanding of how to tackle that area. Essentially, what you should do is walk up and down every street from the Via Frattina to the Via Vittoria in between Via del Corso and Piazza di Spagna—including the fabulous Via del Babuino, which shoots off beside the Piazza di Spagna and goes on its own to the Piazza del Popolo. If you are thorough, and really enjoy each of the shops, you can probably do this in a week. If you are swift, you'll do it in a day. If you are desperate, you can manage in a half day. Obviously, you'll just go into those stores that beckon you. But in case you want help sorting it out, here's our primer:

1. OK, you know all about Via del Corso because you read the section on page 193. You may find the Via del Corso refreshing after you've seen the high prices in the tony shops along the Via Condotti.

2. The Via dei Due Macelli, which runs parallel to Via del Corso but at the top of the shopping trapezoid, is a more high-toned street than Via del Corso. It is considered a fine address, harking back to immediate post–World War II years. Pineider has a shop here (No. 68), one of their nicest shops in all of Italy for papergoods, office items, and stationery chic. The Via dei Due Macelli runs right into the Piazza di Spagna, so it's a good path to walk if you are coming from Via del Tritone. Don't miss McDonald's (No. 46), which is hard to find because it does not have a big sign and is hidden in a pseudo-villa.

3. Via della Vite, the first street running perpendicular between Via dei Due Macelli and Via del Corso, has not quite made it to most guidebooks because it is still an up-and-coming street in this very visible shopping district. But it is not devoid of stores. The Calico Lion (No. 80) is one of the cutest children's stores you will ever see. It's for rich ladies or wild grandmothers, but it is adorable in the old-fashioned way. The handmade bears have personality and flair. The American Book Store is at No. 58, and there's a café called Mario's next door (No. 56) that will do for lunch.

4. The Via Frattina is the first serious shopping street, if you approach from the Via del

Tritone area. It is very different from the rest of the Spanish Steps streets because it still has reasonably priced stores on it and is by no means as hoity-toity as the rest of the neighborhood. Among the finds, there are two identical Castelli shops—a perfume shop that sells a lot of hair clips, earrings, costume jewelry, and fun doodads in the $30–$50 range (at No. 18 and No. 54); Mario Valentino (No. 58 and No. 84); and a smaller Max Mara shop (there is a new one at Via Condotti 46), good for a first look at this respected sportswear company. Be sure to go upstairs to ask for pieces to be shown to you—although this store is not as grand as the big one two blocks away, it's still a nice place to take your business (No. 28). Also see Stefanel (No. 31); Company (No. 126) for *Iceberg* sportswear and hot designer menswear looks; Pollini, the famous shoe store (Nos. 22–24); Fausto Santini with the cute zippy shoes (No. 50); Myricae (No. 36) for faience and incredible pottery; Benetton (No. 44); and Luisa Spagnoli (No. 116), who is an Italian designer specializing in moderately- to upper-priced knits—this store is open "nonstop," which means they don't close for lunch! For the preppy Italian man there is O. Testa (No. 104), which also has a large branch on Via Condotti; for those looking for little silver knickknacks and picture frames, try Artestile (No. 114), which has rather good prices. And, of course, there's a Benetton 012, at the top of Via Frattina at No. 1.

5. Via Borgognona is now the fanciest of the Spanish Steps streets, although those with shops in Via Condotti may argue otherwise. Look for Laura Biagiotti's high-tech mini department store (Nos. 43–44); Gianfranco Ferré at No. 42; and Gianni Versace (No. 41). Visit Lionello Ajo for Sonia Rykiel and many other French big names (Nos. 35–36); and see Cose, which means "things"

and which is celebrated for the "cute little things" they sell—all expensive and chic, like a little cableknit sweater for $800. It's at No. 42, next to Ferré. Céline is here (No. 4) in a villa that looks like an embassy. Franco Maria Ricci—the publisher—is at No. 4d; Fratelli Rossetti is at No. 5a; and Fendi is at Nos. 4e and l. And, of course, our favorite restaurant, Nino, is here (No. 11).

6. Via Condotti is an old-fashioned area and still has many of the big-time shops, where you should at least check the windows. Fogal (No. 55) has no bargains compared with U.S. prices; Beltrami may or may not have better prices than in the United States, but the store is so magnificent that you have to walk into it and browse (No. 19); Max Mara has a bigger and better store at the corner of Largo Goldoni; Gucci is at No. 8 and is huge, with many upstairs chambers that go on forever and sell everything imaginable at rather sensible prices. Don't miss a real find: Cherie, bright red walls inside a townhouse showcase of fashions from Italian *créateurs* (such as Moschino), at Largo Goldoni (No. 43), which is right off Via Condotti, just a sneeze away. Richard Ginori (Nos. 87–90) has a large showroom; Ferragamo is also large, with a men's shop (No. 66) and a women's (No. 73). Cartier (No. 83) has no bargains, nor does Hermès (No. 60). The true find of the street is Campanile (No. 58), for very exciting shoes at affordable prices, although the really snazzy stuff does go over $200. Your $200 just goes further here than almost anywhere else. And if you want to see $200 become meaningless, stop by Bulgari (No. 10).

7. Two cross streets are musts: Via Mario de Fiori (for Ken Scott at No. 114) and Via Bocca di Leone, with Valentino (No. 16) and Miranda, for Italian handknits (No. 28). This is where you should be on the alert for

the street vendors who sell the "Louis Vuitton" bags you've been looking for. We did some hard bargaining and came away with the large Speedy tote for $50 cash, American. We did take a good bit of verbal abuse while we were bargaining, mostly along the lines of: "If all customers were like you, my children would starve." But that was part of the charm of it all.

8. Piazza di Spagna has the American Express office, the Anticoli Gloves Factory (No. 22), and a stretch of fancy leathergoods stores, as well as Genny, the small but luxurious outlet for this line (No. 27). Maurizo Righini (No. 36) is very high-end, with leathers and furs and luggage and some shoes and scarves, and they readily offer you the *détaxe* (a shock) —but the prices are very steep. Pier Caranti (No. 43) is slightly more reasonable, with good buys in the belts in the $50 range.

9. On the other side of the Steps, near the corner of Piazza di Spagna, you'll find the small and dark Via del Babuino. You'll see the light quickly when you discover all the goodies, from Emporio (No. 140) to Missoni (No. 96) to Giorgio Armani (No. 102). Romani (No. 94) has a lot of shoes and bags and accessories that are the latest styles; many are by designers, many are not. Don't miss the Granmercato Antiquario Babuino, which is a minimarket of silver and antiques dealers with little booths—much fun and very elegant, but not so elegant that you can't browse comfortably. This street is crammed with interior design showrooms and fabric houses, lighting experts and antiques shops.

# Size Conversion Chart

## WOMEN'S DRESSES, COATS, AND SKIRTS

| American | 3 | 5 | 7 | 9 | 11 | 12 | 13 | 14 | 15 | 16 | 18 |
|---|---|---|---|---|---|---|---|---|---|---|---|
| Continental | 36 | 38 | 38 | 40 | 40 | 42 | 42 | 44 | 44 | 46 | 48 |
| British | 8 | 10 | 11 | 12 | 13 | 14 | 15 | 16 | 17 | 18 | 20 |

## WOMEN'S BLOUSES AND SWEATERS

| American | 10 | 12 | 14 | 16 | 18 | 20 |
|---|---|---|---|---|---|---|
| Continental | 38 | 40 | 42 | 44 | 46 | 48 |
| British | 32 | 34 | 36 | 38 | 40 | 42 |

## WOMEN'S SHOES

| American | 5 | 6 | 7 | 8 | 9 | 10 |
|---|---|---|---|---|---|---|
| Continental | 36 | 37 | 38 | 39 | 40 | 41 |
| British | 3½ | 4½ | 5½ | 6½ | 7½ | 8½ |

## CHILDREN'S CLOTHING

| American | 3 | 4 | 5 | 6 | 6X |
|---|---|---|---|---|---|
| Continental | 98 | 104 | 110 | 116 | 122 |
| British | 18 | 20 | 22 | 24 | 26 |

## CHILDREN'S SHOES

| American | 8 | 9 | 10 | 11 | 12 | 13 | 1 | 2 | 3 |
|---|---|---|---|---|---|---|---|---|---|
| Continental | 24 | 25 | 27 | 28 | 29 | 30 | 32 | 33 | 34 |
| British | 7 | 8 | 9 | 10 | 11 | 12 | 13 | 1 | 2 |

## MEN'S SUITS

| American | 34 | 36 | 38 | 40 | 42 | 44 | 46 | 48 |
|---|---|---|---|---|---|---|---|---|
| Continental | 44 | 46 | 48 | 50 | 52 | 54 | 56 | 58 |
| British | 34 | 36 | 38 | 40 | 42 | 44 | 46 | 48 |

## MEN'S SHIRTS

| American | 14½ | 15 | 15½ | 16 | 16½ | 17 | 17½ | 18 |
|---|---|---|---|---|---|---|---|---|
| Continental | 37 | 38 | 39 | 41 | 42 | 43 | 44 | 45 |
| British | 14½ | 15 | 15½ | 16 | 16½ | 17 | 17½ | 18 |

## MEN'S SHOES

| American | 7 | 8 | 9 | 10 | 11 | 12 | 13 |
|---|---|---|---|---|---|---|---|
| Continental | 39½ | 41 | 42 | 43 | 44½ | 46 | 47 |
| British | 6 | 7 | 8 | 9 | 10 | 11 | 12 |

# INDEX

## About the Authors

**SUZY GERSHMAN** is an author and journalist who also writes under her maiden name, Suzy Kalter. She has worked in the fiber and fashion industry since 1969 in both New York and Los Angeles and has held editorial positions at *California Apparel News, Mademoiselle, Gentleman's Quarterly*, and *People* magazine, where she was West Coast Style editor. She writes regularly for *Travel and Leisure;* her essays on retailing are text at the Harvard Business School. Mrs. Gershman lives in Connecticut with her husband, author Michael Gershman, and their son. Michael Gershman also contributes to the *Born to Shop* pages.

**JUDITH THOMAS** is a designer who began her career working in the creative and advertising departments of Estée Lauder and Helena Rubinstein in New York. Previously she was an actress in television commercials as well as on and off Broadway. In 1973 she moved to Los Angeles where she was an art director for various studios while studying for her ASID at UCLA. She later formed Panache and Associates, a commercial design firm. She is currently involved in developing and marketing new trends in building design for MPS Systems. Mrs. Thomas lives in Pennsylvania with her husband and two children.